ACCESS ALL AREAS

Acknowledgements

BBC Books would like to thank Clodagh O'Donoghue, Ed Booth, Moira Ross, Richard Thomson, Mark Saben, Jo Wallace, Kate Lawson, Francesca Palmer, Jennie Milward-Oliver, Charlotte Brookes, Claire Callaghan, Kim Winston, Saj Patel, Kat Hebden and everyone on *The Voice UK* production team.

This book is published to accompany the television series entitled *The Voice UK*, first broadcast on BBC1 in 2012.

The Voice UK is produced by Wall to Wall Television Productions, which is part of the Shed Media Group. The Voice is developed by Talpa, the company of Dutch media entrepreneur John de Mol. The original format is owned by Talpa Content B.V. and licensed worldwide by Talpa Distribution B.V.

Executive Producer: Moira Ross
Series Producer: Ed Booth
Series Editor: Clodagh O'Donoghue
BBC Commissioning Executive: Jo Wallace

10 9 8 7 6 5 4 3 2 1

Published in 2012 by BBC Books,
an imprint of Ebury Publishing.

A Random House Group Company

Text by Tim Randall
© Wall to Wall Television Productions 2012

Design by ClarkevanMeurs Design
© Woodlands Books 2012

Photography by David Venni, Guy Levy and Phillip Marriott © BBC 2012

Apart from the following pages: 24–27 © Talpa; 43 (left) by Noel Vasquez/Getty Images for Extra, (centre) by Jamie McCarthy/WireImage, (right) by Jason LaVeris/FilmMagic all © Getty Images; 86–87 © Talpa; 121 (top) by Michael Ochs Archive, (bottom) by CBS Photo Archive both © Getty Images; 122 (top) © Valley Music Ltd/Rex Features, (centre) by Cummings Archives/Redferns and (bottom) by Terry O'Neill both © Getty Images; 123 (top) © Mirrorpix, (centre) © Bettmann/Corbis, (bottom) © Photoreporters Inc/Rex Features; 124 (top) © Richard Young/Rex Features, (centre) © Photoshot/Getty, (bottom) © BBC ; 125 © Tomjones.com LLC

Tim Randall has asserted his right to be identified as the author of this Work in accordance with the Copyright, Designs and Patents Act 1988

The Random House Group Limited Reg. No. 954009

Addresses for companies within the Random House Group can be found at

www.randomhouse.co.uk

A CIP catalogue record for this book is available from the British Library.

ISBN 978 1 849 90485 8

The Random House Group Limited supports The Forest Stewardship Council (FSC®), the leading international forest certification organisation. Our books carrying the FSC label are printed on FSC® certified paper. FSC is the only forest certification scheme endorsed by the leading environmental organisations, including Greenpeace. Our paper procurement policy can be found at www.randomhouse.co.uk/environment

Commissioning Editor: Lorna Russell
Project Editor: Laura Higginson
Designer: Toby Clarke – ClarkevanMeurs Design

Printed and bound in the UK by
Butler Tanner and Dennis Ltd

To buy books by your favourite authors and register for offers, visit www.randomhouse.co.uk

ACCESS ALL AREAS

BEHIND THE SCENES ON BRITAIN'S BIGGEST NEW TALENT SHOW

TIM RANDALL

BOOKS

CONTENTS

THIS IS

Four of the biggest names in music are looking for incredible singing talent to compete for the title of *The Voice*. Only the most unique and distinctive voices will make it to the filmed auditions and get to sing for our celebrity coaches. It was back in September 2011 that the call first went out inviting the UK's most talented singers to come and audition.

The advert continued: 'Please only register for the open auditions if you are an artist with real talent and an amazing voice.' From the word go it was clear this was a singing competition with a difference. For once the emphasis was on awesome vocal ability as opposed to cringe-making comedy performers or fame-hungry wannabes who use their looks to get by. This was about one thing and one thing only – the voice.

'Only the most unique and distinctive voices will make it to the auditions and get to sing for our celebrity coaches'

One of the biggest international hit formats in recent years, *The Voice* was created and first produced in Holland by media entrepreneur John de Mol's company Talpa. Having launched with record ratings in the USA earlier in the year, there was already a buzz around the UK version and the response from the shout-out was immense. From a whopping 25,000 applications, around 17,000 hopefuls sang their hearts out at auditions

THE VOICE!

during October and November. In a bid to win a place at the filmed Blind Auditions they were asked to prepare a contemporary song and popular choices included Beyoncé's 'Halo', 'Grenade' by Bruno Mars, and, perhaps unsurprisingly, everything and anything by

Adele, but more often than not 'Rolling In The Deep' and 'Someone Like You'.

After much speculation in the media as to the identities of the celebrity coaching panel, the dream team of chart queen Jessie J,

'When I went on set for the first time I was so excited – I couldn't believe the scale of it'

REGGIE YATES

legendary crooner Sir Tom Jones, will.i.am of The Black Eyed Peas and The Script frontman Danny O'Donoghue were revealed, alongside the show's presenting duo Holly Willoughby and Radio 1's Reggie Yates.

Meanwhile behind the scenes, Julian Healy, *The Voice*'s designer, was creating a 3D computerised model of the set. The actual building process began in December in a warehouse in Bristol and in the second week of January it arrived at BBC TV Centre on a series of 40ft lorries via the M4 motorway.

It took around 30 people to load and install the structure into Studio One (where *Strictly Come Dancing* is also filmed), and for the first time ever a set was positioned diagonally across the space, allowing the elongated stage to form a diamond shape pointing towards the coaches' oversized red chairs. As band rehearsals began, the finishing touches were being made to the show's iconic giant fists clutching microphones, which had been carved by hand from polystyrene and sprayed with eight coats of car paint to give them the necessary high-end finish.

Co-host Reggie Yates was suitably impressed by what he saw: 'When I went on the set for the first time I was so excited because I walked around the back and down those stairs to the front of the stage like the singers would do and I couldn't believe the scale of it. I got a real buzz of excitement. I was like: "Oh my, this is actually happening." Because it's such a huge show and when I watched the American programme I was just so excited by how different and fresh it was compared to other TV shows. So to be fronting the British version is just awesome!'

The Blind Auditions

Sitting with their backs to the stage, the four coaches must each choose ten artists for their team. Their decision is based solely on vocal ability. If they like a singer they press their 'I Want You' button to turn their chair. If more than one coach turns, the artist then has the power to choose who they want to mentor them.

The Battles

Each coach divides their team into duos and chooses a song for them. The duos battle it out on stage in front of the studio audience and the coach can only choose one artist per duo to proceed to the live shows.

The Live Shows

The artists compete to make it to the final. Every week the TV audience helps the coaches decide on who stays. In the final, each coach will have one artist remaining – but only one will win a recording contract and be crowned 'The Voice UK'!

HOLLY **WILLOUGHBY**

GOLDEN **GIRL**

'Can I sing?' muses Holly Willoughby. 'I would say I have the lethal combination of having all the confidence but none of the ability. So I sing all the time but I am, in fact, terrible. So much so, my stylist said yesterday spending time with me is like hanging out with those mice in the film *Babe*. Because every so often I just burst into a squeaky out-of-tune version of some random song.

'My first foray into singing on live TV, against my will of course, was on Saturday mornings when this little girl was supposed to come on and do 'Get The Party Started' by Pink. Anyway the music began and she just looked at me, sheer panic in her eyes and I thought – you're not going to be able to do this are you? So I went over to her and she gave me another look that said: "You've got to sing this with me." At which point I started to sing, she didn't, and I ended up doing the whole song by myself. As no doubt the nation reached as one for their remote controls to mute their televisions.'

Sitting outside in the middle of the doughnut-shaped building at BBC TV Centre during a break in presenting duties, Holly insists on *The Voice* she'll be leaving the singing to the professionals.

'I am in awe of the voices on this show. The talent is of such a high standard and you think: "Blimey, where have you all been hiding, how come you haven't been discovered yet?". I don't know how the coaches have managed to just pick ten for their teams – I would've put all of them through.'

While she has rubbed shoulders with pop stars aplenty on shows such as *CD:UK*, *Celebrity Juice* and *This Morning*, it's the starry line-up on *The Voice* that has made Holly go weak at the knees.

'Sometimes I feel like I am in Madame Tussauds and it has come to life a little bit. I think Jessie J is incredible. She's really young yet has such a wise head on her shoulders. And I think we have seen a different side to will.i.am, he's so passionate about music yet he's utterly hilarious as well.

'I can hardly look at him because he's just so cute'

'Tom, well, I can't just call him Tom. It doesn't feel right. He has to be either Tom Jones or Sir Tom. Tom doesn't feel like a big enough name for him. When he comes out with stories about Frank Sinatra or Elvis, well, you can't argue with that kind of experience can you?

'I sing all the time but I am terrible'

'Meanwhile, Danny, he struggled with knock-backs and rejection for a long time so if anyone knows what it's like to be a jobbing singer and the frustrations that come with it then it's him. And he's just so handsome...' she adds, with a dreamy sigh. 'I can hardly look at him because he's just so cute. And so much taller than you'd expect. When you go and stand next to him you're a bit like – oh hello, you can pick me up and carry me around for a bit! You're gorgeous...'

REGGIE YATES

HEY MR DJ

As the host of the Official Chart on Radio 1, Reggie Yates knows a thing or two about what it takes to succeed in the music business. He's had a front row seat as the likes of Adele and Gaga have taken on the world, not to mention his stints presenting *Top Of The Pops*, his Saturday afternoon Radio 1 request show and a sideline running one of the coolest monthly club nights in London.

'It goes without saying that it's all about the voices on this show, but on top of that the winner is going to need to be an individual. Which is brilliant to be able to say about a talent show because so many TV talent shows are just so formulaic. Whereas *The Voice* is about finding someone like you have never seen before and that's what makes it so exciting and real. For a start it's not about embarrassing performers and it's not about people who have sob stories that make good television. The power is in the performance on this show. It's just about who can make a song their own and nurturing that talent. This opportunity is just awesome when you think about it.'

Meanwhile, co-host Reggie is keeping his hankies at the ready, as *The Voice* can be an emotional experience for everyone involved.

'I'm a big brother so I am good at being a shoulder to cry on. The emotion we get backstage with the families makes the show even more special. I love meeting the families, you can learn a lot about a performer from the family around them. I get nervous for the singers but not for myself. I have been doing television for 21 years now, so yes you get a little buzz when you go on stage but I don't get too nervous. I am a great believer in doing programmes that I feel passionate about. I am so passionate about *The Voice*. I saw this show when it was first on in America as I was out in LA at the time and I was really intrigued by it all. Then when the call came through, it all felt so surreal.

'I'm Barry White in the shower'

His dulcet tones can also be heard as kiddie favourite Rastamouse, the animated reggae-playing rodent, but it's mention of his turn competing on

'I'm a big brother so I am good at being a shoulder to cry on'

Comic Relief Does Fame Academy seven years ago (he came fourth, by the way) that makes Reggie squirm. 'You had to bring that up didn't you, man?' he grins, shaking his head. 'When I sang it was for charity and it was a long, long time ago. I wouldn't describe myself as a singer but I gave it my best shot, it was for a good cause. How would I describe my singing voice? Like the sound of two frogs making love. But I'm Barry White in the shower!'

INTRODUCING
TEAM VOICE

Welcome to *The Voice*! The nation's media was out in force for the show's official launch, held at a hip central London hotel back in February. One by one the coaches, followed by Holly and Reggie, walked the red carpet before gathering together to strike a group pose for the very first time. 'We're like a big super-band!' joked Jessie J – with her hair in a plaited bun and wearing a long printed dress – as the gang pouted for the mass of assembled photographers and film-crews. Afterwards there was a press conference followed by the screening of a sneak preview of the show. And judging by the enthusiastic whooping at the end, everyone had been seriously impressed by the talent on offer!

'THERE'S A FINE LINE BETWEEN DIVA AND SURVIVAL' JESSIE J

Last year, such was the demand for all things Jessie J that the release of her debut album, *Who You Are*, was brought forward by a month. Meanwhile her UK number ones 'Price Tag' and 'Domino' have become hits Stateside, where 'Party In The USA', originally intended to be a tongue-in-cheek anthem for herself, was an instant chart smash for Disney tween Miley Cyrus – to date the song has clocked up a whopping 271,618,743 hits (and counting) on YouTube.

But the rise of Jessie J is no overnight success. Despite gaining notoriety online (where she was spotted by Chris Brown's manager and booked as his support act), four years earlier her label had gone bust before any of her material could be released, and a girl-band venture had also come to nothing. As if those disappointments weren't enough, while attending the prestigious Brit School she'd suffered a minor stroke months before graduating and was forced to drop out. But these knock-backs didn't dent Jessie J's ambition and, if anything, made her even more determined to succeed.

the things I've learnt. And I'm realising how exciting that is on *The Voice*. If I'd been asked to do this six months into my career I would've said "I'm not sure", because I still feel like I'm queuing up for the ride myself. But a year later I feel I'm ready to bring what I can to the table and put my voice across. To be able to have an opinion and be part of finding some new talent. I'm not here to judge anyone, as I hate being judged, so being called a coach for me is spot on. I feel like I am here to represent a generation that needs to be heard.'

She was 'blown away' by the number of different vocal styles on show during the Blind Auditions: 'There was such an array of different sounds, that was the most surprising and the nicest thing for me. But not being able to see the performers really throws you off, I almost want the audience at home to have their eyes closed as well when they're watching it so they can see how hard it is. Honestly there were times when I was convinced it was a man and then I'd press my button and turn round and, yep, it's a woman.'

'I am here to represent a generation that needs to be heard'

'I've had to hustle hard to get where I am today. So many people have stepped on my journey and now I'm on the other side of it helping other people with all

When coaching her team she feels connected to 'each and every one of them' because she can put herself in their shoes.

'It's so important that they realise this is one of the biggest opportunities they'll ever have. You know, I didn't have this opportunity to be on TV with the whole of the UK watching. It's amazing. I knew I was always going to be someone who would get emotionally attached to my team because that's the kind of person I am. A lot of my group are quite young and some of them have been through some tough stuff and I have to take that on board. I think I've always been attracted to artists with an emotional reasoning behind whatever they do. And I care about helping them understand what's going to come next and how to deal with it, based on my own experience.'

The 24-year-old singer-songwriter has also been instilling the importance of resilience and, above all, hard graft into Team Jessie J.

'You shouldn't ever celebrate anything you didn't have to work hard for. I think that's a very important lesson to learn early on. I've always said my motto is never expect, never presume, always work hard and always be true to who you are. And that's what I'm going to drill into them. You've got to step up to the plate.

'No-one cares if you're ill. No-one cares if you have had a bad day. When people turn on their TV they want to see you give an amazing performance. If I go to see someone on tour, I don't care if they've been on 80 dates. Your mind doesn't think about that, your mind thinks "I want the best performance". Like when you go out to a restaurant, you want your meal to be just as good every time you go. And if it isn't you moan about it but if it's great you don't think about it. It just becomes normality and that's sadly what the music industry is. Great has become normal, bad has become

reactionary. Consistency is probably one of the biggest things in this game. So, you know, you have to keep yourself consistent and you have to look after your voice. There's a very fine line between diva and survival and you have to put yourself first,' she adds, nodding to herself thoughtfully.

'The core is the voice and the singing and the performance. But you do all of a sudden have to learn how it feels to have people pick you apart and have an opinion on how your hair looks, and your eyebrows and how skinny you are and if you sweat. It's just like the world all of a sudden thinks they can own that.

'My motto is never expect, never presume, always work hard and always be true to who you are'

'I was saying to my team yesterday that everyone goes through it. You're not the only person so don't feel sorry for yourself. Be realistic, you're human beings, you're going to get upset and you're going to cry. I've been papped crying, because sometimes I cry. And they're like – Jessie's having a breakdown. No, I'm a girl, girls cry. I was tired, I'd been on planes for three days straight, I hadn't slept and I missed my family. I was having a moment. It's normal, deal with it.'

The Essex-born BRIT award-winner's real name is Jessica Cornish (the J stands for 'different things on different days') and it's

her parents she credits with her phenomenal success. 'Whenever I felt like I didn't know what I was doing, it was my mum and dad that I went to. They were the ones I could turn to and say I need to talk to you or I need a cuddle or I need to understand what's going on.

'You've also got to soak up what's going on around you. I remember watching Beyoncé do a sound check at the VMAs and she was just so on it and so polite. It's all about manners. You know, don't ever think you have the right to treat people differently just because you sing. Or because you've earned a bit of money or you're top five in the chart. Like, know yourself. Make sure you keep your feet on the ground. I always find it very strange when people treat me differently, but then I suppose the artists I've been around work hard but they also say please and thank you. That's why I'm such close friends with people like Ellie Goulding and Pro and Tinie, people that respect their fans and their upbringing and aren't up their backsides basically. Because, let's face it, that's really not a great place to be!'

TEAM
JESSIE J

THE VOICE

From the moment the US coaches belted out a rousing rendition of the Gnarls Barley hit 'Crazy' during the opening episode, *The Voice* began trending on Twitter and the top dogs at NBC became aware they had a hit in on their hands. That debut episode blasted to No. 1 in the ratings with 11.8 million viewers, beating established shows like *Glee* and within weeks there was already talk of a second season.

rising country star Blake Shelton and all-round 'muso' Cee Lo Green, as the expert coaches.

'The blind auditions are actually what sold it to me because it was a fresh idea,' says Cee Lo, who had also performed on *The Voice of Holland*. 'No-one was in a rush to be the bearer of bad news or to be the judge or superior to anyone, because we are artists

'The four of us coaches have such a love-hate relationship. As soon as somebody comes up on that stage and they're really good, the gloves come off' BLAKE SHELTON

Adapted from the Dutch TV show *The Voice of Holland* (which itself had become a ratings-topper), several elements played their part in making the show a success – the coaches sitting in big red chairs with their backs to the contestants so they could hear them without seeing them, the focus on singing as opposed to sob stories, and the power-struggle as the coaches scrap among themselves to bag the best singers for their team.

These format twists all helped the first season capture a peak of 14.4 million viewers, as did the selection of vocal superstar Christina Aguilera, Maroon 5 frontman Adam Levine,

OF AMERICA

ourselves. When we considered it coaching and mentoring as opposed to judging I was like: "I can do that!"'

The winner of season one was an early favourite, baby-faced soul-singer Javier Colon. The father of two from Connecticut took home a $100,000 prize plus an album deal with Universal Records. During the final he teamed up with his coach Adam Levine to perform Michael Jackson's 'Man In The Mirror' and the pair have remained in contact.

'I knew from the first moment I heard him sing that he would win. He's the best singer

ever,' says Adam. 'I saw this show as a way to bring in new talent and give people a second, third or even fourth chance.'

Indeed, Javier was no stranger to the music business. Having picked up a deal with Capitol Records in 2002, his contract was terminated four years later and despite a frustration that his career was stalling, he wasn't ready to throw in the towel just yet.

'Things were tight, we were getting by but barely. Our kids have always had everything they needed, but you want to be able to give your kids the world and that was something we weren't able to do before *The Voice*.

'The Voice actually kind of changed my life. I want to continue to be excited by this whole strange amazing journey' ADAM LEVINE

'It's amazing what a little time, luck and a TV show can do to turn things around. And not just to turn my career around, but to turn around the outlook of my family, turn around the path we were on. I'm so grateful to *The Voice* for really not only just changing my life, but all of our lives in my family.'

Other finalists such as runner-up Dia Frampton, singer-songwriter Vicci Martinez and bald tattooed rocker Beverly McClellan embarked on a nationwide tour alongside Javier, and have all been working on solo material. In December 2011 Dia released her debut solo album, *Red*, which featured a duet with her coach Blake Shelton. She also picked up a support slot on his recent tour. 'Blake was a very active coach and even after *The Voice* ended he's still been very much in my life and extremely helpful, even with my music career. I'm lucky because he has been supporting me every step of the way.'

Meanwhile, Cee Lo's last-woman-standing, Vicci Martinez, has been in Berlin working on her album with The Cardigans' Peter Svensson. 'Since the tour ended life has been a very crazy ride,' she says. 'It's so awesome to have these producers and writers wanting to work with you. I definitely feel this show has made me way more focused and boosted me.'

And it's not just the contestants who have found *The Voice* to be a life-changing experience. 'What I found last season through *The Voice* was that I kind of love helping these guys out. Every step of the way was really fun and I looked forward to going to work the next day,' says Adam Levine.

'It was this new, exciting thing and a totally different angle I'd never explored before. So *The Voice* actually kind of changed my life. I want to continue to be excited by this whole strange amazing journey. The show really inspired me last season and I want to be inspired all over again.'

All four coaches have returned for the second season – again hosted by Carson Daly – which kicked off in February in a prime-slot following Madonna's comeback appearance on the Super Bowl with a whopping 37.6 million viewers, making it the highest rating non-sports show for six years. And it looks as if the rivals all picked up where they left off when filming began.

'The four of us coaches just have such a love-hate relationship,' says Blake Shelton. 'We're all high-fiving and drinking together, but as soon as somebody comes up on that stage and we hear them and they're really good, the gloves come off. It's like: "Did you just say that to me? Why did you say that, dude? I just wanted to get that girl. Oh, okay!" Then you're back and everything's good again.'

In an online interview to promote the second run, a battle-ready Christina Aguilera seemed to be thinking along the same lines. 'Me

and the boys had a blast last season. We all formed such a relationship throughout it all. But I'm ready this year. I'm bringing my game face. It's on!'

On a more serious note, she added: 'It's beautiful to work with such eager and hungry talent, truly amazing voices coming from all different genres and tones and techniques. The younger they are the less technique they have and there is more to sort of mould, and then the older they get the more technique they bring to the table. It's so fun to see the versatility and how many artists come together for this show. It's inspiring. How can I walk away from this experience and not be inspired?'

Since his victory, Javier Colon has released a new album *Come Through For You* (which features duets with Natasha Bedingfield and his mentor Adam Levine), he's appeared on *The Tonight Show with Jay Leno* and performed at a benefit gala with Stevie Wonder. He's spent most of this year fulfilling a lifelong ambition by headlining his own *Come Through For You* tour across the States.

'Winning season one has offered me so many opportunities I never thought would be possible,' he says. 'The future is a lot brighter than it was before. I was this close to hanging it up – and now the sky is the limit.'

'THE MOST IMPORTANT THING FOR ME IS INDIVIDUALITY' TOM JONES

The term 'legend' is often bandied about too easily, but with a career spanning six decades and still going strong, there is surely no other way to describe the music industry veteran dubbed 'cooler than an igloo' by his fellow coach will.i.am.

He has constantly changed his game to remain at the top, from being bombarded with knickers on stage in Las Vegas, to his reinvention with 'Kiss' and 'Reload', to raising the bar for renditions of gospel spirituals with his recent critically acclaimed album *Praise & Blame* (only Eminem's latest kept him from No. 1). He's played working men's clubs in South Wales, hosted his own TV show on both sides of the Atlantic, been knighted by the Queen and over the years has performed with everyone from Robbie Williams to Elvis Presley.

So when asked how he would've fared if *The Voice* had been around when he was starting out, Tom Jones breaks into a smirk. 'I think I would've done alright,' he replies, with a trademark twinkle. 'Especially with *The Voice*, because I am known as The Voice, so there you go. With a show like this I would've been in my element.'

And he's in no doubt about what it will take to win this year's competition. 'The most important thing for me is individuality. What I've been looking for is personality coming through when they're singing someone else's song, rather than just copying a record. It doesn't have to be a big voice, but it has to be an individual voice.

'The other thing for me is light and shade and to think about the song before you sing it. Read into the lyrics and find a way to connect with them. Think about what they mean to you. Like an actor does for a role. That's what makes great actors and that's what makes great singers, as far as I am concerned. That they have an individuality and that their take on it is different to someone else's. I think I made good choices for my team and I feel I have the most individual voices and the strongest voices in the competition.

'You learn as you go along that when people like what you do it gives you a confidence'

'I think like most Welsh people, I like strong singers with character in their voices, that's what gets us. Luckily my voice came pretty naturally because in those working men's clubs, when I used to be there, you had to learn to project because some places didn't have microphones, so you had to make yourself heard. Especially when there are so many big voices in

Wales, you've got to make them sit up and listen. To try and sing in those clubs without projecting would've been impossible because they wouldn't have given you the time of day. So you learnt that you've got to hit it hard when you get up there and it's the same on this show. You need confidence in yourself and in your voice. You have to think – well I know I can sing and I'm going to prove it right now. If you go "Oh no, are they going to like me?", well, you've got a tough job then.'

Having a mentor is also key to a successful recording career and Tom's original manager Gordon Mills (who penned his debut smash 'It's Not Unusual') proved to be the singer's guiding light.

'Gordon had come home from London to see his mum who lived five miles away from where I was born. You didn't meet many people in show business in South Wales, not in those days anyway. He came in and saw me perform at this working men's club. If that hadn't happened I don't know how much longer it would have taken for someone to show me the way.

'It's important that you have somebody alongside you that is musical. Some managers are not musical, they are just business managers. But when you have someone like Gordon Mills, he was a musician so he knew what he was talking about. Because I'm always open to criticism, I'm not like it's my way or the highway. That's how you can ensure longevity, by listening and taking advice from those you trust around you. My first record producer was called Peter Sullivan and he heard things in me that maybe I didn't know were there. He got me to try this and to try that. So I was very lucky to have him too.

'But at the same time you should realise that these people are just suggesting things, it doesn't mean to say they are always right. So you've got to stay true to yourself, but take advice and at least try things and give them a shot. Don't get swayed too much by trends either, not too much. You don't want to be sticking out like a sore thumb, but you've got to

'One night I was beaten by a ventriloquist – she wasn't very good either. The dummy was great though'

have something about you that people like. I started singing as a child, so you learn as you go along that when people like what you do, it gives you a confidence. It gives you the courage to know when to stick to your guns. That's something you learn over time, it really is.''

With a career that has encompassed struggles as well as the highs, Tom understands only too well the frustration felt by those leaving the show during the Battles.

'I know there's more these people can do in the future, but as far as I'm concerned it's about who's the strongest person on the night, it has to be. They are hard decisions to make and it's a shame that someone has to go home. But that's the nature of the competition and I have to try and explain that just because they don't get through to the next round, it doesn't mean they haven't got something special.

'If you are confident in yourself you've just got to shrug your shoulders and go, well, it wasn't my night. When I was starting out I used to go to competitions in clubs, we used to call them Go As You Please, that was the term and I used to go up against other people. I mean, one night I was beaten by a bleeding ventriloquist.' Recounting the story is making him laugh. 'And she wasn't very good either. The dummy was great though, she stole the show...

'So when something like that happens you can go – that's the reason why. If you can focus on the reason why then you'll get through it and if anything it'll make you even more determined. It certainly didn't do me any harm.'

Read more about the life and times of Tom Jones on page 120

33

'1 KNOW WHAT THIS CRAZY JOURNEY CAN BE LIKE'

DANNY O'DONOGHUE

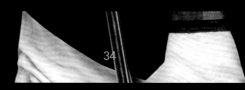
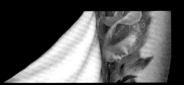

On the surface it looks like success came pretty quickly for The Script – but Danny O'Donoghue is a man who has paid his dues. After his boy-band, Mytown, failed to set the world alight, the charismatic singer wound up in the US spending a decade as a songwriter and producer (with The Script's Mark Sheehan) working alongside R 'n' B luminaries such as Dallas Austin, Boyz II Men and The Neptunes.

Performance at the 2010 Meteor Awards (the Irish equivalent of the BRITS) even beating their idols, U2.

'This is the type of stuff that I think I can share with these people [on *The Voice*], because I know what this crazy journey can be like. I know what it's like to be a nobody and then be thrust straight into shaking hands with Paul McCartney and opening for U2 in your home town. They

'I have been told no more times than I've been told yes in my career'

But it was when The Script's critically acclaimed self-titled debut album stormed to number one in both Ireland and the UK, that Danny, guitarist Mark and Glen Power (the band's drummer) found their careers hurtling skywards.

'It has been quite fast for us. We went from playing the Sugar Club in Dublin in 2008 to 46 people – we literally sold 46 tickets – to three years later selling out 60,000 tickets, about two miles down the road at the Aviva National Stadium. Words cannot describe what that amount of people singing your songs does for the human spirit.'

Their soaring anthems also garnered the attention of U2 and Paul McCartney, who both asked the band to open for them. The trio went on to win Best Live

are real pinch-me moments and it plays with your head. We were scared about getting on stage because our heroes were literally coming on after us.

'We have been very blessed that we've had a lot of people who have taken an interest in our career at various stages. U2 and Paul McCartney individually would've taught us many different things. Paul McCartney was so cool and also interested in how we felt going from playing small clubs and pubs to that. He taught us about how to bring 80,000 people onto the stage with you and that it's not only about your performance, it's about your storytelling as well. He said you've got to invite people in and tell them a story about the song, then we watched him do just that on stage and you could've heard a pin drop. I was like, oh man, that's a piece of advice I am going to take to the grave with me. So now I'm telling everyone stories beforehand!

'The thing those experiences have taught me, above everything, is the importance of professionalism. At this level now on *The Voice* everyone is a great singer, but are they great professionals? Because that's the side of the industry that nobody ever sees. That actually diva qualities – requesting obscene things for your rooms, being difficult backstage – is bad for you. It's bad for the people around you to deal with and it isn't a great career move.

'We have always left a great name wherever we went, you know, U2 taught us that. That wherever you go you shake everybody's hand, you say thank you to everybody – it doesn't matter if they are making you a coffee or if they are in charge of the whole thing. You have to treat everyone the same. I've been in the industry now for 14 or 15 years, and the people that were the tea-makers are now the decision makers. And you're looking at one. I used to make the tea. I was one of those people that artists were assholes to and the funny thing is it comes around full-circle again. Now those same people are calling me up wanting to make music and if they hadn't burnt those bridges all those years ago then who knows what we might've done together.'

The Irish rockers' multi-platinum-selling second album, *Science & Faith*, again hit the top spots in Ireland and the UK. Meanwhile over in the States 'Breakeven' had been a huge smash (peaking at No. 12) and selling a rather impressive 2.5 million copies. But the reaction to the new album exceeded everyone's expectation: 'When *Science & Faith* got to No. 3 on the Billboard charts, that was a big highlight. You can't argue with that.'

With these achievements under his belt, Danny wants to share the love and give other musicians a leg-up on *The Voice*.

'This show is the first show that I can actually put my hand on my heart and say it's about talent above everything else. There is an untapped pool of talent in the UK that won't do TV shows for fear of being ridiculed, this show puts all of that at ease and puts it back into musicians' heads that it's all about the music. The level of talent on the first audition day of *The Voice* for me was better than the final of any other show, literally just on the first day. So it was hard to know when to turn around at first because everyone had something special. I couldn't really say what I was wanting to hear, but they just sang and I heard it and I turned around, you know?'

'Words cannot describe what that amount of people singing your songs does for the human spirit'

The 31-year-old Dubliner wants his team to take positives away from their time on the show, regardless of how far they proceed.

'It is hard to say no to people because you are really letting someone down. But I have been told no more times than I've been told yes in my career and I'm still sitting on *The Voice* being a coach. You need to have true belief in yourself. If you take that no on board 100 per cent it's going to defeat you as a person. But if you go, actually, I'm going to prove you wrong. That's the right attitude. But it is hard, there's no denying it. For me whenever I picked myself back up it normally wasn't me picking myself up, it was other people. Your family, your friends and everyone around you. So your social circle is a big one to help you get over stuff like that.

'I feel for these guys, it's nerve-wracking stuff and I totally understand people are going to be nervous. Whoever is going to stand up on that stage is going to wobble a little bit. But that's the whole part of this, you don't have to be the finished article yet, there's plenty of time for that. It doesn't matter who you are, it's an intimidating arena. If I was to get up there I'd still be all over the place – and that's the honest truth.'

TEAM
DANNY

FINDING

What is your number one warm-up exercise?

'It may sound strange but humming is the best way to start your vocal warm-up, followed by lip rolls or trills. A humming exercise loosens the mucus off the vocal cords and the lip roll/ trill warms the voice with no stress on the vocal.'

Sometimes I find myself out of breath when singing – why is that?

'If you find yourself running out of breath when singing, you're more than likely not using your diaphragm. Try the following exercises. Lie flat on your back, rest your head on a book to stop your head from falling too far back thereby restricting your air flow. Place a book on your stomach and as you inhale push the stomach slowly out for a count of five, hold for two counts and exhale for a count of five. Then slowly increase the count to ten, inhaling, hold for two counts and exhale to a count of ten. Repeat the exercise ten times slowly increasing the count.'

JAY HENRY

YOUR VOICE

As every singer knows the voice is a precious instrument – here some of the show's vocal coaches reveal their tricks of the trade...

What is the best way to strengthen my voice?

'The best way to strengthen your voice is to warm-up and vocally exercise daily. You must use your voice to perform regularly. Your voice and the strength of it has lots to do with technique, but also confidence. So there's no point doing loads of vocal exercises at home and not going out and using what you have learnt. Confidence plays a big part, so get yourself down to the pub karaoke competition, singers' jam night or join a function band and make some money too!'

MARK DE LISSER

What is your number one remedy for a sore throat?

'Steaming (head over a bowl of hot water or a commercial steamer from chemists) is the best remedy. It lubricates the vocal folds which sit on top of your windpipe and helps to clear the lungs of goo. Other remedies such as throat sweets can be comforting, but many can make you dry. Drink two litres of water a day.'

MAUREEN SCOTT

Should I sing if I have a cold?

'A cold that causes your speaking voice to change may be the result of swollen vocal folds and to sing on these may cause further irritation. If there is any sensitivity, pain, inflammation or infection it is crucial to avoid singing until it has completely cleared.'

JAI RAMAGE

Is it true consuming dairy products and alcohol isn't good for my vocal cords?

'Milk and dairy produce have been associated with increased mucus production, but there's medical evidence that reports no influence. Some people are lactose-intolerant and people need to be aware of their own symptoms and reactions. Drinking alcohol dehydrates the body and hydration is good for singing, our vocal cords and general health. Also you may well think you're a fantastic singer when you're drinking, but you may also think that wearing a traffic cone on your head is a good look.'

JULIET RUSSELL

FLIPS AND BELT?

The Voice's much-used vocal terminology, explained...

LICKS
Primarily a melodic phrase or hook. It can be used to refer to improvisations or ad-libs. It can also be used to describe someone's style or vocal signatures
....

RUNS
A series of notes, often fast, requiring vocal agility or dexterity
....

FLIPS
A sudden change between registers. Movements from chest to head voice and vice versa

ATTACK
How the sung note starts. It can be soft, hard, clean, raspy (Britney Spears: 'Oh baby baby') or any kind of attack the singer chooses
....

TONE
The unique tonal quality of a singer, which can be manipulated but is essentially the vocal tone we are born with
....

BELT
This is using the chest voice to create a loud energised vocal sound. Very powerful and emotive

✦ ✦ ★ ★ STAR SOUNDS ★ ★ ✦ ✦

Our vocal experts work with the best in the business, but who has *really* impressed them?

'**Mika** is very clever, he is always working on improving and expanding his technical ability. He has emotional commitment to his material and can perform a two-and-a-half-hour show every night, plus travelling miles each day, and still be secure vocally. **Björk** is technically impressive, she uses her voice extremely efficiently and delivers a fantastic performance at every concert. She can sing in so many styles which is reflected in the material she has written.' MAUREEN SCOTT

'The vocalists I've sung with that have truly impressed me are **Stevie Wonder** for vocal range, power and control. And **Luther Vandross** for tone, expression and vocal agility.' JAY HENRY

'**Jessie J** at 16 was the most naturally gifted singer that I have ever worked with. Her tone and agility were just so well developed for such a young singer. And her ability to connect emotionally was just so spot on. Believable every time.' MARK DE LISSER

'I loved working alongside **Ruby Turner**. She always sings from the heart and her voice is rich and soulful. She has a wide vocal range and creates great dynamic contrasts.' JAI RAMAGE

'I like singers who have a lot of character in their voices and are distinctive. **Damon Albarn** is a really interesting vocalist. He has an amazing range and his voice sits within so many musical styles, without ever losing its unique identity.' JULIET RUSSELL

'I REMEMBER ME WHEN I WAS TRYING, STRUGGLING, DREAMING' WILL.I.AM

Rapper, producer, musician, hit-maker and hip-hop renaissance man, will.i.am is hard to categorise. Best known as the front man of multi Grammy award-winning chartbusters The Black Eyed Peas, he's also made headlines for his work with Michael Jackson ('That felt like a dream') and as the mastermind behind Cheryl Cole's solo success (she is signed to his label). But perhaps what no-one had

whole experience, it's much better than I thought it was going to be actually. It's the bomb.com!

'The UK is very special to me because I am in fact more successful in the UK than I am in America. I think you get my artistic sensibility more than in the States so I like coming to the UK. You get me. And I like being around every single one of the other coaches. Danny is super-cool, he thinks

'There is amazing talent in the UK, it's a smaller country than where I come from but it's quality over quantity, that's what I find here'

latched onto about will.i.am before *The Voice* was his sense of humour, which turns out to be as infectious as The Black Eyed Peas' beats that have sold a mind-boggling 58 million singles worldwide.

'I like being silly. You know, I've been doing entertainment for a while now, 15 years in the Peas. When I'm outside of the Peas I feel kind of outside of my camp, so *The Voice* is a new journey for me. I was always shy, I can't just turn myself on like a switch, but I find it easier to do here than back home. I think Jessie has helped bring out my silly side and just to have fun. So maybe people have seen another side to me – because I'm having a good time. I've enjoyed the

about music every second. We'll be sitting eating a sandwich and he'll be like: "Man, I've just written a song about the sandwich!" It's an honour to be around Tom, hang out with him and pick his brain, and Jessie is a real pick me up, like 1000 volts of energy. We've had a lot of fun times.'

It has also been an emotional experience for will.i.am, 37, who's been reduced to tears several times. 'It's emotional listening to everybody's stories, hearing their abilities. Everybody has a dream and if I put myself into that situation I start to remember me when I was trying, struggling, dreaming. So it's all very emotional if you're open to that.'

One thing that hasn't surprised the self-confessed Anglophile is the talent on offer on these shores. 'There is amazing talent here in the UK, it's a smaller country than where I come from but it's quality over quantity, that's what I find here in the UK. And this show is so cool because we are just focusing on the voice. Singing is all that matters and having your back turned is the ideal way to just listen to somebody. Because nowadays the state of the industry is that they'll pick a person just because she's hot and even if she can't sing they're like "We'll figure that out later, we'll fix that."

'So this is great, it just takes it back to what it is supposed to be and that's why I am so honoured to be part of the show, because we are taking it full circle. I think that's a beautiful way to go about it. And of all the people we saw only one person didn't sing good, which is pretty miraculous really. That out of over 100 people only one person was okay as opposed to great. That's pretty cool.'

William James Adams was raised by his mum in a housing project in East LA and from an early age was encouraged to follow his passion for music. As a teenager he became a rapper on the club scene and after meeting lifelong friend Apl.de.ap at school, they formed The Black Eyed Peas in 1995 alongside Taboo, recruiting singer Fergie in 2003 for the smash 'Where Is The Love', which was a worldwide No. 1 and the biggest selling single of the year in the UK. Meanwhile 2012 saw the release of his latest album as a solo artist, *#willpower*.

'Really the main thing is believing in yourself and how fragile the moment is – you can be liked and hated, here today and gone today.

So you could be a great singer but your behaviour could change how long you last and how much you learn. So just try to own as much of where you are going, be responsible for it all, the good and the bad. Don't rely on your management or your label, especially nowadays, take on all that you can do yourself.

'Don't rely on your management or your label, especially nowadays. Take on all that you can do yourself'

'That's the differentiating factor between me and the other coaches – Jessie sings wonderful, Danny is an amazing singer, songwriter and producer and Tom Jones is a legend. But they have managers. I don't have a traditional manager. I take pride in the fact I co-manage my group and self-manage and if I can instil that upon my team it would be great. Because that's what I think the artists of tomorrow are – people who can manage themselves, write their songs, produce their songs, market their songs, promote their songs, come up with their own concepts and videos and collaborate with different co-writers and figure out what entertainment is. If I can instil that in them, with the gift they already have, I think they can be phenomenal artists.'

Having worked with stars as diverse as Michael Jackson, Britney Spears, Rihanna, Justin Timberlake and Nicki Minaj (he is currently

collaborating with teen sensation Justin Bieber), will.i.am is an expert on bringing out the best in big name talent.

'I follow my gut through my whole career, sometimes my gut has got me into a rut, but surprisingly it's very rare that happened. I'm doing the show because there's the opportunity to help someone out like I was helped out and if I don't try to make an artist bigger than me, then why am I even here?' He insists the experiences all of his team have gained from the show, will make them better artists in the long run.

'I don't look at it as rejection, I look at it as learning. If you look at it as rejection then you are never going to learn and you are going to get hurt. I've been through lots of turn-downs, got my emotions all rattled up and hopes up, and then you're let down. But as many times as you're let down, when you finally get up you'll be bigger than you would have been if you'd got that first opportunity. So the longer you wait, the bigger you are going to be when you finally get there. That's the truth for everything.'

TEAM
WILL. I. AM

The atmosphere in the studio is electric, the capacity audience has been whipped into a frenzy by break-dancing warm-up man Stuart Holdham and there's more anticipation the air than a penalty shoot-out and the Olympic one hundred metres combined. Yes, it's that tense. Over the next four days more than one hundred hopefuls are singing for a place in the next stage of the competition and this is how the lucky chosen 40 did it.

So, it's day one. The coaches are ready in their outsized red chairs facing away from the stage. The crowd has fallen silent and a lone figure with a shock of purple hair makes her way down the steps and into pole-position for the very first blind audition. She takes a deep breath, the band bursts into life and within seconds Aundrea Nyle from London is rockin' the studio with a belting rendition of Gnarls Barkley's

BLIND

As seen from our front-row seat, here's the lowdown on how the final 40 artists sang for their lives and won their places on the coaches' teams...

'Crazy'. There's no doubt she's won over the crowd (who are out of their seats), but can she win over the coaches?

will.i.am closes his eyes, Danny's nodding along, Jessie's looking thoughtful, but it's Tom Jones who presses his button and spins around: 'I love the vibrato of your voice, spot on. And you sang it differently to Cee Lo, you did your own thing and I loved that,' says Tom. 'You were the first one out so you must've been nervous. Come on, give us a kiss!' Cue swoons from ladies-of-a-certain-age amongst the audience.

> ## 'You were the first one out so you must've been nervous. Come on, give us a kiss!'
>
> TOM JONES

AMBITION

Next up is flat-cap wearing David Faulkner from Wales, who storms his way through Stevie Wonder's 'Superstition'. All the coaches swivel around. Danny and Tom even give him a standing ovation. will.i.am calls his voice 'spectacular' while Jessie explains he's the reason she wanted to do the show – to find a person who can really 'saaaaang' (she says it in an American-style twang so we're not sure how to write that down). Tom plays to David's patriotic side: 'We Welsh people should stick together.' Frankly we have no idea which way this is going to go and it doesn't look like David does either. He's lost for words. 'What should I do?' he asks the audience, cue lots of screaming out of the coaches' names.

One woman helpfully shouts out: 'Brucie!' Maybe she's turned up for the wrong show? But David has made up his mind – he's choosing Jessie J!

'It just feels weird to be gigging with shoes on'

VINCE FREEMAN

The coaches also start wrangling over 20-year-old Joelle Moses whose knockout 'Rolling In The Deep' bowls them over. She clamps her hands to her head. 'I'm messing up my face, my make-up's running,' she laughs between sobs, as Jessie J runs onto the stage for a big hug. In a final bid to win her over, Jessie also suggests they could share shoe collections (Joelle is wearing some impressive heels), but the Londoner has made her decision: I've got to go with my gut instinct, and it's telling me will.i.am.'

Danny and Tom enjoy Leanne Mitchell's take on 'If I Were A Boy' and press their buttons at the same moment, when she hits a particularly big goose-bumpy note. Leanne eventually opts for Team Tom, but Danny's luck of the Irish comes into play when 23-year-old Bill Downs' soulful take on 'She Said' by Plan B (plus unexpected falsetto) wins him over.

Next up there's Matt and Sueleen, a duo from Canterbury. He's got a big furry beard and they sing a folky, haunting version of The Beautiful South's 'A Little Time'. Both Tom and Jessie swivel for them and (we can't believe they are about to do this) the 34-year-old couple decide to flip a coin for it. The audience hushes.

Matt tosses. Who's it going to be? It's heads ... which means they join Team Tom Jones.

Student Hannah Berney's vocal acrobatics on Gaga's 'You & I' go down a storm – Tom tries playing the Welsh card again, but this time loses out to a triumphant Danny. Meanwhile Dudley based 'singing barmaid' Jenny Jones begs for 'Mercy' and picks will.i.am as her coach. This excites him so much he actually moonwalks across the stage to give her a hug.

Next the band start playing 'Like A Virgin'. Tune! It's a fresh, soulful beat version and all the coaches turn their chairs. When Danny comments it was a flawless performance, 21-year-old Vince Kidd from Surrey starts crying (someone get some tissues on this set!). will.i.am says he put a whole 'bunch of soul-sauce' into a classic pop song, but in the end Vince chooses his idol Jessie J, and leaves the stage a red-eyed but very happy bunny.

Team Tom's next signings are 19-year-old Ruth Brown who impresses with a fierce 'When Love Takes Over' ('Anyone with lungs

Yourself', which totally rocks Danny's boat. As does Mancunian David Julien who tries his luck on The Script's 'The Man Who Can't Be Moved': 'The way you sang it had the same spin and emotion in it as when I wrote it. Fantastic.' Which must be a huge relief for David who reveals he quit his job in a supermarket to audition.

like that is good enough for me!' says The Legend) and Sam Buttery, from Birmingham, puts his own stamp on Adele's 'Set Fire To The Rain': 'I heard a little bit of me in there to be honest,' Tom reveals to a delighted Sam.

'It had the same spin and emotion as when I wrote it'

DANNY O'DONOGHUE

There's a cool mash-up from cheery 20-year-old Londoner, Max Milner, it's The Beatles's 'Come Together' mixed with Eminem's 'Lose

J. Marie Cooper struts around the stage as she powers through 'Mama Knows Best' (much to Jessie's amusement). All the coaches buy into it. Jessie J stands up and throws in some moves of her own and, sensing that the competition is on, Danny and Tom also leap up and start applauding. Jessie tells J Marie that her voice is 'Redonkulousо!' while Tom insists her vocals were 'on fire'. The audience are calling out the coaches' names, and the 27-year-old goes for will.i.am, who says: 'In your voice I heard a personality, a pain and a love for the craft.'

Team Jessie J rules when 32-year-old Cassius Henry opts for her over Danny. But Danny ups the stakes when he bags goateed Vince Freeman, who rocks out to 'Sex On Fire'. It looks like Vince has forgotten to put shoes on? Yep, he's barefoot. 'I just don't like performing with shoes,' he explains to the intrigued coaches. 'I started playing in my bedroom barefoot so it just feels weird to be gigging with shoes on.' Jessie asks if he's got nice feet. Vince laughs: 'Nope' I've got webbed feet.' Jessie likes this and compares his feet to those of a frog.

When 17-year-old performing arts student Frances Wood from Wakefield breaks into The Black Eyed Peas 'Where Is The Love' will.i.am's face doesn't move a muscle. Will he or won't he like it? He isn't giving

Next it's 34-year-old Toni Warne, from Norfolk, with a heartfelt performance of Will Young's 'Leave Right Now'. Danny calls it even better than the original while Jessie says Toni could teach her something about singing: 'Your tone is timeless,' she adds. Toni explains she lost her hair when she was 22 and as a result her confidence as a performer melted away. Picking her dream coach is a hard decision for Toni – she's a huge fan of Tom Jones, but says listening . to Jessie's album gave her such a confidence boost and that's why she's choosing her.

anything away. But on the very last note he turns his chair with a big naughty schoolboy grin on his face. What a little tease he is!

Tom is instantly won over by Barbara Bryceland's classy rendition of the Rolling Stones' 'Wild Horses': 'You have a wonderful voice and I am proud to have you on my team.' Grinning from ear to ear 47-year-old Barbara looks pretty chuffed about it as well. Meanwhile Jessie's 'tummy starts burning' and she whips her chair around when she hears 25-year-old session singer Kirsten Joy steam her way through Emili Sande's 'Heaven'.

When Heshima Thompson takes to the stage, all the coaches press their buttons to see the 'actor, singer, dancer' throwing in a few smooth Jacko style moves as he belts out Taio Cruz's 'Dynamite'. After much deliberation, he opts for Team will.i.am. As does 24-year-old Liverpudlian, Jay Norton, whose unique voice and riffs make Aloe Blacc's 'I Need A Dollar' truly his own.

Danny is quick to bag 33-year-old John James Newman following his crowd-pleasingly Bobby McFerrin and Eliza Doolittle mash-up. Jessie J falls for Ruth Ann St Luce's vocal acrobatics on Leona Lewis's 'Run', saying Ruth Ann's technique has left her speechless (surely a first?).

It's Ireland versus the USA as both Danny and will.i.am attempt to lure Bo Bruce, a 26-year-old singer songwriter from Wiltshire, to their lineup. They agree her voice on 'Without You' by Usher has shades of Dido and The Cranberries' Delores O'Riordan. 'I don't know what to do,' she says stroking her head as the audience shriek out the names of both interested parties. After much soul-searching and head-scratching Bo takes a deep breath … Dan's her man!

Mum of two Lindsey Butler's country-tinged version of 'I Don't Wanna Talk About It' rocks Tom's boat and she calls Danny cute when he compliments her 'amazing' voice. But before The Script frontman gets too big for his boots, she adds: 'But not as cute as Tom Jones!' Cue a satisfied smirk from The Legend who jumps up and punches the air in delight.

'You have a wonderful voice and I'm proud to have you on my team'

TOM JONES

Northern Ireland's Ben Kelly sports a striking Jedward style blond quiff (could he be the long lost third brother?) and he's barely sung a note of 'Rocket Man' before will.i.am turns around, swiftly followed by the other team-leaders. They each make their bid for his talents, Ben tells the boys they're great before pointing at Jessie: 'But this girl is for me!' Jessie J also snaps up Jessica Hammond, from Belfast, after hearing her unique acoustic version of her own song 'Price Tag', saying she loved that the 17-year-old had put her own spin on it. Teenagers Indie & Pixie, a best mate duo –

singing 'Perfect' by Pink – also choose Jessie over the other coaches. Even though an excited will.i.am raves about their performance too.

'You took something that's dear to me and sang it in your own way, which was beautiful'

WILL.I.AM

'I'm pretty overwhelmed' sighs young lifeguard Aleks Josh, when both will.i.am and Danny press their buttons during Jason Mraz's 'I'm Yours'. He looks quite shaken so Jessie sits on stage with her arm around him, while he focuses on the task hand. 'I'm not very good at explaining, but I feel it has got to be Danny,' he decides with a relieved grin. Musician Murray Hockridge's soulful vocals on 'You Give Me Something' also appeal to Danny, who adores his 'smokey old wisdom tone'.

The next singer looks familiar ... OMG it's Deniece Pearson from Five Star! Okay, you need to be over 35 and have a love of mid-80s pop to know this, but alongside her brothers and sisters (usually wearing shiny matching jumpsuits) they enjoyed sizeable chart success. She takes on 'Fighter' by Christina Aguilera, which captivates Tom who loves the strength of her voice: 'What hit me more than anything is your tone and power and that's why I want you on my team.' The coaches don't seem to recognise Deniece, but they are probably too young, too old or too American!

The studio suddenly feels like an intimate jazz club as 19-year-old dance student, Kate Read, draws everyone in with her gentle delivery of 'True Colours'. Jessie calls her tone 'tingly' and curls her fingers in a grrr kind of way to emphasise the point. Kate says she thinks of her mum when she sings which hits a nerve with will.i.am who says everything he does is for his mom: 'She's my inspiration so thank you for mentioning your mom on The Voice,' he adds. What a polite chap – and as a result Kate picks him.

'I know that tune!' exclaims will.i.am after busker-student, Sophie Griffin, sings Estelle's 'American Boy', a song will.i.am co-wrote. She jumps up and down with joy when she nails him as her coach. Next is rosy-cheeked 21-year-old Emmy J Mac, from Bath, who has the pick of all the male coaches when her 'Put Your Records On' tickles their fancies. 'It's make your mind up time,' says Jessie, doing her best Cilla Black on Blind Date impression, before a relieved-looking Emily finally opts for Team Danny.

Things go name-dropping crazy between will.i.am and Tom Jones when 28-year-old Adam Isaac dazzles them with mellow Stereophonics' anthem 'Maybe Tomorrow'. Adam explains he also likes to rock out and asks if his potential mentors would be up for that. Which leads to Tom finally playing the Elvis card (yes!) saying he used to rock out all the time with Elvis. There's a huge cheer from the crowd at this – can will.i.am compete? Yes, he can! He plays the rockin' out with Michael Jackson card (nice move), which also gets a round of applause. But it's only Adam who can

decide whose name-dropping has done the trick – and he chooses Elvis's mate Tom Jones.

Tom scores again when new mum Denise Morgan sings her heart out to Sarah Bareilles' 'Love Song'. 'You're on my team, Sweetheart!' he calls out with a grin. When impish 17-year-old Becky Hill appears on stage no-one expects such a huge belter of a voice. She's singing John Legend's 'Ordinary People' (written by will.i.am about the break up of a relationship). Jessie is 'blown away' by the standard of the performance, while will.i.am is clearly moved: 'You took something that's dear to me and you sang it in your own way, which was beautiful.'

Becky is gobsmacked by the feedback. 'I've got a bit of a decision to make,' she says, thoughtfully. Eventually she opts for Jessie as her ideal mentor, but will.i.am's luck is in when

he secures singer-songwriter Tyler James who sings a soulful 'Sitting On The Dock Of The Bay', which impresses the Black Eyed Peas star. 'You are so cool,' he tells Tyler as he leaves the stage.

Ed Sheeran's 'The A Team' is the next tune, delivered with tenderness by 26-year-old Jaz Ellington, who is a gospel-loving soul singer from South London. The whole audience sways along with him and will.i.am says he sings like 'you just fell out of the sky 'n' stuff.' When Jessie J asks him to sing something else for them, Jaz begins an acapella version of 'Ordinary People', which makes Jessie cry. The song's writer will.i.am is very moved, tears stream down his face and, without hesitation, he signs up an overwhelmed Jaz for his team. What a moment! So, that's the end of the Blinds – it has been emotional. Now where are those pesky tissues?

Hannah Berney

I've been gigging professionally for four or five years now, but I didn't know I had the ability to get this far. So I think all that emotion came through at once and my head was buzzing about everything that was going to happen. Then suddenly Tom was asking me what my mum was called and there I am standing on the stage with everyone looking at me and I just couldn't remember her name. I'd totally blanked out.

The 20-year-old cheerleader from Wales has always wanted to be a popstar and pays her way through university by gigging. She was so gobsmacked when chosen at the Blinds that she forgot her mum's name!

'My nan went to the same school as Tom Jones and my mum was born in the same town, so when Tom and Danny both turned round I got really emotional (because I'm half Irish as well) and I was crying with relief more than anything. This show is such a great opportunity.

'I was crying with relief more than anything'

When I walked off stage I was still in a state of shock and I'd got make-up streaming down my face. My mum was watching backstage and when I got there she said: "Hello, you might not know me? My name is Charlie." I was like: "Sorry Mum!"'

THE VOICES THAT INSPIRE ME

I love Gavin DeGraw. He has an amazingly gravelly soul voice. I'm also a massive fan of Alison Krauss – her voice is unbelievably moving and every time she sings you know exactly what she means.

TEAM DANNY

Tyler James

The 30-year-old Londoner was once signed to the same label as his best friend Amy Winehouse, but it didn't work out for him. After a difficult year, Tyler is rediscovering his love of performing...

'The reason I decided to do this, to be honest, was because last year was the worst year of my life and I felt like now was the right time to get back into what I do best and just throw

'This has reignited my passion for what I do'

myself completely in at the deep end. Since Amy died I have been wallowing and when you're grieving you do disconnect from people and it's easy to isolate yourself.

But at the same time, when you lose your best friend it does make you realise life is short and to grab opportunities. So as much as this show is a singing competition, personally it is also about me taking an important step to put myself back out there and to get back some of my confidence.

I haven't sung for a long time and what's amazing is this show really has reignited my passion for what I do. will.i.am noticed something in my voice and I feel privileged that he did. Whatever happens, I'm heading in the right direction in my life now and that's something for which I am very grateful.'

THE VOICES THAT INSPIRE ME

Lauryn Hill. Technically she is amazing, she's a gifted songwriter and most importantly I think it's just about the tone of that voice. She inspires me massively, as do Marvin Gaye and Otis Redding.

TEAM WILL.I.AM

BACKSTAGE PASS

What is it really like behind the scenes when you're a coach on *The Voice*?

That's the question we've been asking ourselves for a while. So when Danny O'Donoghue invited us to spend the day with him as his team rehearsed for the Battles, we jumped at the chance to catch him in action...

It's an early morning start but Danny arrives at the studio in good spirits and is immediately whisked into hair and make-up – where his trademark mega-quiff is sculpted into position...

He entertains the crew with a few tunes in his dressing room... but doesn't react well when someone says their favourite coaches are Tom Jones and Jessie J!

While waiting to be called onto set, he takes time out to strum handsomely. Maybe there will be some *The Voice*-inspired tracks on the new album?

It's time to get up close and personal as his microphone-pack is attached underneath his clothing. Many female members of the crew now wish they'd volunteered for this task...

Danny heads into the studio to oversee his team rehearsals and wisely ignores the sign on the door. No 'ear-protectors' needed on this show!

Some last-minute fine-tuning with Yvie Burnett, one of the expert vocal coaches, before a team pep-talk on what he's expecting from them at the Battles...

Hiding away by the monitors it's all smiles as he checks out how the duos are coming across on camera...

There's a bit of a hair-spray touch-up for the all-important quiff, while being briefed by the production team...

Standing to attention, he supervises another duet run-through and afterwards gets a big hug from one of his artists, Murray Hockridge.

It has been a long day but The Script frontman is still kicking back and enjoying himself. He's about to head off to film some more interviews, meanwhile we're exhausted and need a lie-down. Thanks for having us, Danny!

Vince Kidd

at anything else and I feel ready to get signed now, so hopefully this will be a great platform. I got a publishing deal on the back of two songs I'd written and now I feel ready to put my music out there.

'All I can really do is write songs, sing and put on crazy outfits'

The 22-year-old music-industry songwriter from South London is often judged for his distinctive look – now it's his voice that's making him stand out from the crowd...

'I often get judged on my appearance, so being chosen for my voice alone has been really cool. I think I've got quite a distinctive voice, because sometimes I sound like a girl and sometimes I sound like a fella. It's soulful too and I wanted to be in a gospel choir when I was a kid – that was my one ambition. All I can really do is write songs, sing and put on crazy outfits. I'm not very good

All four coaches turning around at the Blinds was amazing because I respect them all, but I wanted Jessie from the word go. I love her. She comes from a similar background, we have similar influences and I used to go to her gigs in London when she was unsigned, so what has happened to her is really inspiring for me. She's just a really cool pop star with substance to her music – she's totally putting her stamp on it and that's the kind of artist I'd like to be.'

THE VOICES THAT INSPIRE ME

The first artist I fell in love with was Amy Winehouse. That voice was like something I'd never heard before and she really made her pain beautiful. Other inspirations are Boy George and Lauryn Hill.

TEAM JESSIE J

Leanne Mitchell

lucky. But this whole experience has made me realise that I want more. The opportunity means everything to me.

I began singing when I was seven years old and by the time I was 14 I'd made an album. A little while later, my management took me to America to meet lots of bigwigs and that went really well. There was all this hype that the people over there had built up around me, but then the company I was with ran out of money and we couldn't afford to follow everything up. So over the next year or so it all fizzled out.

The 28-year-old singer and vocal arranger from Lowestoft once came close to the big time until her record deal fell through. She now works at a holiday park and is relishing her second chance...

'I love my job at the holiday park, I literally have to sing everything from rock to opera. I get to sing every day for a living, so in that sense I'm really

I've been at the holiday park for 13 years now and I do genuinely enjoy it, but in terms of trying to progress as an artist I'd just lost all faith in people. *The Voice* has given me a bit of fire back in my belly and my mindset has totally changed – now I'm ready to follow my dream again.'

'It has given me a bit of fire back in my belly'

THE VOICES THAT INSPIRE ME

I love Beyoncé's voice and find everything that she is about is so inspirational. I also love the big vocal divas like Adele, Whitney Houston and Celine Dion.

TEAM
TOM JONES

SECRETS OF

The outsized red chairs are as much a part of *The Voice* as the artists and the coaches themselves – but you can't buy yourself one at your local Ikea. Each chair is created from scratch, taking several weeks to build, and when assembled weighs in at a whopping 125kg (around 19 stone). Made of steel for strength, clad in timber, fitted with LED light panels, upholstered with vinyl leatherette and sprayed with red car paint, it takes three days to assemble and install each chair onto the set.

'The chairs were a challenge, to be honest. For a start they are extremely heavy and it takes at least three guys to lift one into position,' explains *The Voice*'s set designer Julian Healy. 'Then to try and get the chairs

'The chairs were a challenge to be honest – they rip around at quite a force and could do some damage!'

THE CHAIRS

to do everything that they are supposed to and do it all in sequence, do it smoothly and do it safely at the press of a button, is quite a complicated computer system. As you can imagine there were lots of nerdy conversations going on about how to do it.

'Luckily we had YouTube videos from the American version so we could see exactly what the chairs were expected to do during The Blinds when they turn. Basically it's on a belt drive so it's what they call ramping up and ramping down. It's very difficult to see to the naked eye, but it starts slowly, gains some speed and then as it comes to rest it slows

down, so you don't get a jolt when it stops. Obviously we wouldn't want to give any of the coaches whiplash.

'When the coach presses the button that isn't a signal for a man in a back-room somewhere to turn it around, the coaches have direct control over their chairs. Although there is an override if that fails, which is done by someone who has line of sight of the coaches at all times, making sure the chairs don't turn when there is someone in the vicinity of them. Because they rip around at quite a force [between 4 and 2.5 seconds] and could do some damage!'

Bo Bruce

The 26-year-old singer-songwriter from Wiltshire has spent years trying to succeed in the music industry, but her big break has eluded her. She's turned to *The Voice* to make it happen...

'I know how hard it is to get a break. I feel I have been in so many label boardrooms and for whatever reason never quite making the cut. There have been moments where I've thought this

'I'd actually managed to move Danny emotionally'

is it, it's happening and then it hasn't and to have to get back on the horse is really difficult after that kind of fall.

Ultimately what bucks me up is my love of singing. So for me the auditions were amazing especially because it appeared I had actually managed to move Danny emotionally. Seeing how much he was into it was incredible. Sometimes I think "I'm skint, I should just give this up and go and pull pints for the rest of my life." And I'd be happy doing that. But then something like this happens and it just scratches the itch.

I feel really honoured to be part of *The Voice* and excited that this many people are finally hearing me sing. Not only is the talent insane, but I don't have an obvious big belting technical voice, it's small and it's quirky, so to have got through it with that knowledge is wicked.'

THE VOICES THAT INSPIRE ME

Sinéad O'Connor, because of the truth and vulnerability of her voice. I grew up with a lot of Barry White around the house and I love the creativity of Björk and Annie Lennox.

TEAM DANNY

Joelle Moses

wasn't going to be enough to move things on. I had to do something big to get noticed – and then I heard about *The Voice*.

'I had to do something big to get noticed'

The 21-year-old West London-based session singer has been working hard behind the scenes recording backing vocals and demos for producers. Now this is her time to shine...

'I came on *The Voice* because I wanted a real chance to showcase my talent. I want to be a recording artist and I've been doing a lot of session work to try and get in there with producers, but it hasn't led to anything. I'm a demo singer, I sing at gigs, in nightclubs, anywhere that will have me really. But recently I realised that just doing the rounds and doing the session singing

Because we share the same birthday, I take a lot of inspiration from Muhammad Ali and the things he said. He was so confident, so sure of himself and he had no doubt in his abilities. In the music industry the knock-backs can make you start to doubt yourself, but when I started to think like him it only reinforced my self-belief.

That's why after I finished singing at the Blinds I just burst into tears. I was so emotional and it was only afterwards that I realised it was because I finally felt accepted.'

THE VOICES THAT INSPIRE ME

Chaka Khan and Whitney Houston are huge vocal inspirations and weirdly they both did 'I'm Every Woman', which I sang at the Battles. They are both incredible icons to me.

TEAM WILL.I.AM

GOING LIVE

However experienced you are, singing live on TV can be a nerve-racking business. Here the coaches reveal their backstage rituals plus tips on how to perform like a pro...

WILL.I.AM

You need to have a 'whatever' attitude. If you start thinking 'Eek I'm on TV!' and start panicking then you are going to fall on your face. If you don't have a sense of being chilled, well, you have to get one. You need to put your worry onto something else, not what you are about to do.

My thing before I go on stage is to stress out about something else – your computer not working, your phone, your dog. Just don't think about the show. Because ultimately you going on stage in front of the world isn't a problem, but so many people make it into a problem and that's when they mess up.

My other performance tip is to sing to someone you know. I remember when Fergie went on tour by herself and she was like: 'I've been touring with you guys forever, will.i.am, I'm nervous.' So I was like: 'Fergie, who is your best friend? You tell her all your problems, yes? She's someone who'll tell you if you've got a bogey on your nose, yes? Then you need to pick out people in the audience and pretend those people are your best friend and sing to them.' Imagining you're performing to someone close to you makes you handle it all so much better psychologically, because they appreciate and understand the real you.

Make sure you do a decent vocal warm up – always sing the highest note you are going to do a few times to make sure you can go there. In my dressing room I always have manuka honey, lemon, ginger and hot water sitting there ready. Make sure the water is hot enough, but not boiling hot.

It's important to get yourself into the zone before a performance but it's not always that easy. It depends on my mood, who I am around and what I've been doing all day. If I've had five hours of phone interviews, where I have been talking about all different kinds of things, then it's quite hard to focus.

Like I went on television recently and my head wasn't in it and I got the words wrong and I was so angry at myself. Before you perform it should all be about you having to go 'Right, I need to get in the zone now' and finding time to focus on that. Because once it has gone wrong it has gone wrong and there's no turning back.

The first thing you've got to do is not think about how many people are watching. You can't start panicking about how many millions are sitting at home watching you, because if you do start to think like that you'll crumble.

TOM JONES

Personally I don't like being in the dressing room too early because then you start over-thinking what you are about to do. Some singers have to have complete silence and they have to concentrate, but I don't. I like to have conversation going on, which means I'm not thinking about the performance and then all of a sudden the music's starting and boom, you're doing it. But at the same time you've got to be well rehearsed, you don't want to be winging anything.

Hopefully you can get a good night's sleep beforehand, without that you can get very edgy. Make sure the air when you sleep is humidified and also drink plenty of water to make sure you don't get dehydrated.

'The first thing you've got to do is not think about how many people are watching'

Avoid alcohol as well. Some people say 'Oh I have a little drink before I go on, it'll give me some confidence' but if anything it's going to slow you down and sap your strength. If you haven't got the confidence to begin with I'm not sure alcohol is going to help.

DANNY O'DONOGHUE

What I need before singing on TV is not to have any distractions. So I always have an hour before a performance where even my mum, friends and relations are not allowed into the room – simply because their excited energy really rubs off. I get excited very easily, so if I've got all that nervous energy around me then I get ten times as nervous. I turn my phone off as well and ignore all outside distractions. So for performing on television my biggest tip is to think about your breathing. You've got to relax. Think serenity and calm. That will help you so much, I promise you.

If you're just performing one song on a TV show, you then need to take time to try and channel the song or the songwriter. If you're doing your own stuff that's the perfect conduit because then you are your own emotion. But when you've got to learn someone else's song you have to make yourself believe it, concentrate on the lyrics and think about what it means to you. Because if you don't believe in the music and the words, you sure as hell aren't going to convince me. And you aren't going to convince the other people who are watching either.

Ruth-Ann St Luce

probably around six or seven when I really got the singing bug and I'd do it anywhere and everywhere, whether it was in my bedroom, the garden or on the front porch. Ever since then I've always wanted to be a singer.

The 17-year-old music student and retail assistant from London has been music-mad for ten years and taught herself to play the piano and guitar. She dreams of singing for a living...

'There was always someone singing in our house when I was growing up. We lived in the Caribbean at the time and my dad taught us lots of songs, usually something gospel or inspirational. I was

'I'm quite shy but I get my confidence when I am on stage'

I think I'm more myself when I sing than when I'm not singing, if that makes sense. I'm quite shy but I get my confidence when I am on stage. I chose to do *The Voice* because I thought I had potential and I just hope that the UK sees that in me. I knew I had a lot to learn, so when I found out who the coaches were on the show I knew they'd be able to give me the guidance I need to develop and grow in the industry. I have learnt so much already about my voice and every second I am just grasping onto information and learning as much as I can. Because this is something I dream about doing for the rest of my life.'

THE VOICES THAT INSPIRE ME

Michael Jackson is very inspiring – even when he was young he knew how to perform and work the mic. I love Whitney Houston and Beyoncé too, their voices take my breath away.

TEAM JESSIE J

The 28-year-old gigging musician from Exeter once supported Joss Stone on tour and would give anything to be booked to play at Glastonbury. He describes life on *The Voice* as a roller-coaster ride...

'Because I'm a laid-back, quiet person people think that I'll play like that as well, but sometimes I like to express myself by rocking out a bit when I'm gigging. I was really pleased when Tom chose the Kings Of Leon's 'Use Somebody' for my Battle song – it's in the right ballpark for me so that was a relief.

I usually play in small bars and clubs, sometimes with a band and sometimes I play acoustic gigs, so to go from that to a TV studio was quite mind-blowing and I did spend a lot of time worrying about it. I wasn't scared about being bad, it was more that music is what I love so my fear was that someone would say I should be doing something else instead. Thankfully that didn't happen.

'You can't stop laughing and your eyes are wide with adrenalin'

Performing on *The Voice* is a bit like when you go on a theme park ride. You are really worried beforehand but you want to see what it's like, then when you get off you can't stop laughing and your eyes are wide with adrenalin. It's just like that – such a cool feeling!'

THE VOICES THAT INSPIRE ME

My favourite artist is Jeff Buckley, his voice is unique and his falsetto encouraged me to try it as well. I really like Kelly Jones too, his voice is so screwed-up and raspy.

TEAM TOM JONES

Max Milner

which have to be sung in a certain way, that have been written by the composer and that's that. Whereas I'd like to be the writer of my own music and stand there with a guitar instead of some ballet shoes. I want people to be able to hear a track and go "Oh yes, that's Max", because I think I've got quite a unique voice.

'I'd like to stand there with a guitar instead of ballet shoes'

The 21-year-old musician from London trained as a dancer and is a singer in his own rock band. He's played lead roles in *High School Musical* and *Footloose* – but now he's ready to go solo...

'Both of my parents have musical backgrounds – my mum's currently playing the lead role in *Mamma Mia* in the West End – so being around theatres and seeing them up on stage has seemed normal to me from a young age.

Don't get me wrong, I've enjoyed being in musical theatre, but when you have a part in a show you get particular songs

What I really like about *The Voice* is it allows you to be looked upon as a recording artist, because I aspire to have a career like Danny and the other coaches. I really respect them because they've all had to work hard for their success. I've always written my own songs and, in an ideal world, I'd like to be able to do what I do with my guitar at home every day, but get paid for it!'

THE VOICES THAT INSPIRE ME

I'm a big fan of John Mayer, he has a massive amount of husk in his voice. I also love the way Paolo Nutini sings in his own accent and is so raspy yet so musical.

TEAM DANNY

Toni Warne

worthy of much more. I wasn't confident enough to look further than the end of my nose.

'My hair went completely and so did every ounce of my confidence'

The 34-year-old mum from Norfolk has been performing since she was a child, but her confidence took a knock at the age of 21 when she lost her hair due to alopecia. Thanks to *The Voice* her self-belief is soaring again...

'Before I lost my hair I wanted to aim as high as I could with my singing. But then my hair went completely and so did every ounce of my confidence and the self-belief that you need to make it in this industry. So I stayed in my comfort zone and I kept doing local pubs and bars. I was still singing, but felt I had to settle for second best because I wasn't

So to then find myself standing onstage at the Blinds with these amazing musicians telling me they loved my voice, wow, that took me by surprise. I really didn't think the chairs were going to turn when they heard me, so I was overwhelmed with emotion and it was the most magical and amazing feeling, I can't explain it in any other way. I really did conquer some fears that night and climbed a mountain I wouldn't have dared go near a few years ago. It has been a long time since I've felt the way I feel now, in fact, I never remember feeling this good!'

THE VOICES THAT INSPIRE ME

Karen Clark-Sheard is the greatest gospel singer ever, she's capable of every possible note and feels every single one of them. Barbra Streisand is another big inspiration – the notes she sings are crazy.

TEAM JESSIE J

HOW WELL DO YOU KNOW THE COACHES?

Is Danny your obsession or do you know
Tom Jones better than he knows himself?

Tick your answers below and turn over to see how Holly and Reggie got on...

1 What is the name of Tom Jones's first British No. 1?
☐ 'Delilah'
☐ 'It's Not Unusual'
☐ 'What's New Pussycat'
☐ 'Sex Bomb'

2 will.i.am produced, co-wrote and featured on which Top 5 single from Cheryl Cole's debut album *3 Words*?
☐ 'The Flood'
☐ 'Fight For This Love'
☐ 'Stand Up'
☐ '3 Words'

3 Before forming The Script, Danny was in an Irish boyband – what were they called?
☐ BoyTown
☐ MyTown
☐ UpTown
☐ Downtown

4 'Every second is a highlight, when we touch don't ever let me go' is a lyric from which Jessie J hit?
☐ 'Price Tag'
☐ 'Nobody's Perfect'
☐ 'Who You Are'
☐ 'Domino'

5 On his 1999 album *Reload*, with whom did Tom duet on the song 'Are You Gonna Go My Way'?
☐ Stereophonics
☐ Robbie Williams
☐ Mousse T
☐ Cerys Matthews

6 In which Steve Carrell movie did will.i.am make a brief cameo as himself?
☐ *Get Smart*
☐ *The 40 Year Old Virgin*
☐ *Date Night*
☐ *Crazy, Stupid, Love*

7 Which of the following singles by The Script stormed to the top of the Irish chart in 2010?
☐ 'Breakeven'
☐ 'The Man Who Can't Be Moved'
☐ 'For The First Time'
☐ 'If You Ever Come Back'

8 Tom appeared in animated form in an episode of *The Simpsons*, but which character was his No. 1 fan?
☐ Marge
☐ Mr Burns
☐ Smithers
☐ Chief Wiggum

9 Jessie J originally wrote her first single 'Do It Like A Dude' with which globally famous artist in mind?
☐ Katy Perry
☐ Miley Cyrus
☐ Rihanna
☐ Sinitta

10 How many dates did The Script play on their *Science & Faith World Tour*, which began in September 2010?
☐ 32
☐ 8
☐ 120
☐ 147

11 When studying performing arts as a teen which of these actors was Jessie J's classmate?
☐ Matt Smith (*Doctor Who*)
☐ James Buckley (*The Inbetweeners*)
☐ Jack Whitehall (*Fresh Meat*)
☐ Robert Pattinson (*Twilight*)

12 In 2009, which will.i.am produced Black Eyes Peas song became the group's first US No. 1?
☐ 'Boom Boom Pow'
☐ 'Let's Get It Started'
☐ 'Don't Phunk With My Heart'
☐ 'Where Is The Love'

8/12

9/12

Have you beaten Holly and Reggie?

1 What is the name of Tom Jones's first British No. 1?
- (HW) ☐ 'Delilah'
- (RY) ☐ 'It's Not Unusual'
- ☐ 'What's New Pussycat'
- ☐ 'Sex Bomb'

2 will.i.am produced, co-wrote and featured on which Top 5 single from Cheryl Cole's debut album *3 Words*?
- ☐ 'The Flood'
- ☐ 'Fight For This Love'
- ☐ 'Stand Up'
- (RY) (HW) ☐ '3 Words'

3 Before forming The Script, Danny was in an Irish boyband – what were they called?
- ☐ Boy Town
- ☐ My Town
- (RY) (HW) ☐ Up Town
- ☐ Downtown

4 'Every second is a highlight, when we touch don't ever let me go' is a lyric from which Jessie J hit?
- ☐ 'Price Tag'
- (RY) ☐ 'Nobody's Perfect'
- ☐ 'Who You Are'
- (HW) ☐ 'Domino'

5 On his 1999 album *Reload*, with whom did Tom duet on the song 'Are You Gonna Go My Way'?
- (RY) ☐ Stereophonics
- (HW) ☐ Robbie Williams
- ☐ Mousse T
- ☐ Cerys Matthews

6 In which Steve Carrell movie did will.i.am make a brief cameo as himself?
- ☐ *Get Smart*
- ☐ *The 40 Year Old Virgin*
- (RY) (HW) ☐ *Date Night*
- ☐ *Crazy, Stupid, Love*

7 Which of the following singles by The Script stormed to the top of the Irish chart in 2010?
- (HW) ☐ 'Breakeven'
- ☐ 'The Man Who Can't Be Moved'
- (RY) ☐ 'For The First Time'
- ☐ 'If You Ever Come Back'

8 Tom appeared in animated form in an episode of *The Simpsons*, but which character was his No. 1 fan?
- (RY) (HW) ☐ Marge
- ☐ Mr Burns
- ☐ Smithers
- ☐ Chief Wiggum

9 Jessie J originally wrote her first single 'Do It Like A Dude' with which globally famous artist in mind?
- (RY) ☐ Katy Perry
- ☐ Miley Cyrus
- (HW) ☐ Rihanna
- ☐ Sinitta

10 How many dates did The Script play on their *Science & Faith World Tour*, which began in September 2010?
- ☐ 32
- ☐ 78
- (RY) ☐ 120
- (HW) ☐ 147

11 When studying performing arts as a teen which of these actors was Jessie J's classmate?
- (HW) ☐ Matt Smith (*Doctor Who*)
- (RY) ☐ James Buckley (*The Inbetweeners*)
- ☐ Jack Whitehall (*Fresh Meat*)
- ☐ Robert Pattinson (*Twilight*)

12 In 2009, which will.i.am produced Black Eyes Peas song became the group's first US No. 1?
- (RY) (HW) ☐ 'Boom Boom Pow'
- ☐ 'Let's Get It Started'
- ☐ 'Don't Phunk With My Heart'
- ☐ 'Where Is The Love'

Matt & Sueleen

Normally we play pubs, universities and quite a lot on the festival circuit. We've certainly never performed in front of a studio audience before, but strangely it has just felt really natural. Obviously you have to try and keep the nerves under control, but because everyone has been so great behind the scenes, *The Voice* has just felt like a really positive experience.

The 34-year-old couple from Canterbury have been singing together for eight years. Matt, a chef, and teaching assistant Sueleen have been determined to enjoy every moment on *The Voice*...

'We live in a very musical household and if we're not playing music then we're listening to music. We rehearsed for *The Voice* on the floor of our kitchen because it's the warmest room in the house and we also found ourselves in the bathroom quite a lot, either sat on the bath or singing away on the loo, because the acoustics in there are so good.

'It's great to break out of your comfort zone'

We've been encouraged to have fun and to enjoy ourselves as much as possible out there on stage, so that's what we've tried to do. It's great to break out of your comfort zone and test yourself a bit. The more rounds we get through the more the confidence grows – and the more we feel like we can take on the world!'

THE VOICES THAT INSPIRE ME

We really like The Civil Wars who won a Grammy this year – they are a male-female duo like us and their harmonies are outstanding. They sound both beautiful and haunting at the same time.

TEAM
TOM JONES

The 17-year-old student and busker from Country Tyrone is currently studying for her A-levels, but she is convinced that singing is her only career path…

'I've been singing forever, since I was no age really and it's all I want to do. I'm always singing at home and our next-door neighbours say they can hear me all the time. I think they like it, well, they haven't complained just yet, put it that way. I'm also studying music and performing arts at school and I busk and I do gigs in tiny pubs with a friend,

usually to about three people and mainly empty chairs and tables. But it is great to just get out there and do it because I really think it helps you grow as a performer.

'I busk and I do gigs in tiny pubs usually to about three people'

I adore being on *The Voice* because I love being with people who love music as much as I do. When I'm at home everyone tells me to shut up about it, but being here with likeminded people is like being on *Glee* or something! I've already gained so much knowledge and experience. I'd never worked with a vocal coach before, so that has been an amazing opportunity. You learn so much about your voice and now I can do things I truly never thought I could.'

THE VOICES THAT INSPIRE ME

I could listen to Ed Sheeran all day and the fact that he writes and raps as well is incredible. I love Nicki Minaj and Beyoncé too – they are both totally amazing.

TEAM WILL.I.AM

WE GOTTA

It really was a good (good) night when the coaches showed everyone how it's done with their storming rendition of The Black Eyed Peas' smash 'I Gotta Feeling'. In fact, Danny O'Donoghue is still getting his head around it. 'I can honestly say it's the weirdest thing that has happened to me in my life. To sit at the piano and have Tom Jones there, will.i.am to the right and Jessie J behind me and we're all singing and doing harmonies together... If there are things you think you'll never do in life, this was one of them. When you say it out loud it sounds like some crazy night in a hotel.' As for the song's co-writer, will.i.am, it's an experience that's going to stay with him too: 'I never thought I would ever hear Tom Jones sing our song, but it was amazing. It's a great memory and it's now in my head forever!'

FEELING!

From Australia to Albania it seems *The Voice* is taking over the planet. Here's the inside track on just a handful of them...

MEXICO

vision – lives in a tiny village with his parents. His father became a celebrity himself, for sobbing away each week in the studio audience during his son's performances. So much so that in the final Ivan sang a specially written ballad titled 'Don't Cry Father'...which of course just made his dad sob even more!

Mexico
When school caretaker Oscar Cruz was named *La Voz...Mexico* – clinching a recording contract and a new car – no-one was more thrilled than his coach, Latin music superstar Alejandro Sanz. And it seems the multi-Grammy award winner (pictured second from left), who hails from Spain, fell a little bit head over heels for Mexico too.

'My participation in the programme has left me with a deeper knowledge and love for this country than the one I had before,' he revealed after the final. 'I leave here [in Mexico] a lot of my heart.'

Ukraine
Winner Ivan Hanzera gained the affection of the Ukrainian TV audience with his pitch-perfect yet heartfelt vocals. The accordion playing 23-year-old – who only has 30 per cent

PORTUGAL

Portugal
There's an extra coach to impress on *A Voz de Portugal* where brothers Nélson and Sérgio Rosado, better known as rock duo Anjos (Angels) share the mentoring duties. Unfortunately for the siblings, the fact there's two of them doesn't mean they get double the amount of artists on their team!

SWEDEN

Sweden One of the country's most famous faces features on the coaching panel of *The Voice Sverige*. Carola Häggkvist's debut album, *Främling*, remains the country's biggest ever seller and she's entered Eurovision three times, winning in 1991 and most recently coming fifth in 2006. Meanwhile in Denmark, there's Aqua's Lene Nystrøm (of 'Barbie Girl' fame) and *The Voice of Germany*'s coaching line-up boasts homegrown pop queen, Nena.

Ireland Westlife's Kian Egan has been making headlines on *The Voice of Ireland*, notably for his passionate opinions and his rivalry with fellow coach, Brian Kennedy. Also on the panel are singing violinist Sharon Corr and The Blizzards' Bressie. 'Brian comes from a different place in music than I do,' Kian explained in an interview. 'He might not necessarily agree with a lot of things that I agree with and vice versa, but that's what makes the show so versatile.'

Holland London born tattoo-artist Ben Saunders, who grew up in Hoorn, came, saw and conquered on the first season of *The Voice of Holland*, which marked the format's TV debut and became the country's highest-rating talent show ever. He rocked out to Kings Of Leon's 'Use Somebody' at his audition and three chairs turned around within the first few seconds of his vocal. When the fourth coach didn't turn immediately

another coach (an excited VanVelzen, pictured with Ben, who went on to become his mentor) pushed the button for him.

HOLLAND

In the final 'Tattoo Ben' crooned 'If You Don't Know Me By Now' which went on to top the charts, as did the track 'Killed For A Broken Heart'. His tattoo shop is being managed by his dad as Ben is now a full-time musician. 'I haven't changed, but people around me treat me differently. When I walk down the street I get people greeting me every hundred metres or so – but I am still just a country boy from Hoorn!'

Bulgaria At 17 years old, Steliana Hristova is the first-ever female winner of *The Voice*. Over the course of the Bulgarian final, the shy girl with the crystal-clear voice zoomed up the popularity stakes from fourth place to eventually take the crown.

BULGARIA

Becky Hill

I ended up doing the song I went on to do at the Blinds, John Legend's 'Ordinary People' and I had the lyrics written out on my palm, that's how last-minute I am. But I do take my singing seriously because it's the thing I love more than anything. It just feels so natural to me.

'I take my singing seriously because it's the thing I love more than anything'

The 18-year-old sixth form student and weekend barmaid from Worcestershire writes all the music for her own band and says singing is her first love...

'The thing about me is I'm a very last-minute person or I'm still a kid, I haven't worked out which yet. So it was only by chance that I managed to make it to the open audition, I'd been working in a bar until three that morning and was really tired and convinced I'd sleep through my alarm. Thankfully a friend called me first thing which woke me up and I caught the train to Birmingham to give it my best shot.

I had no idea will.i.am had written the song until just before the Blinds when I looked it up on the internet with my mum. Then I realised it could either work for me or against me. Afterwards he explained it was all about dealing with the end of a nine-year relationship and when he was telling me that I was nearly in tears.'

THE VOICES THAT INSPIRE ME

I find Stevie Wonder very inspirational. His voice is always in tune and he experiments with different notes and can go to them with such ease. Ben Howard is another favourite at the moment.

TEAM JESSIE J

David Julien

The 23-year-old singer-songwriter from Manchester plays the piano and guitar. He used to work the nightshift at a supermarket, but gave it up to take part in the show...

'I've never done anything like this before because most music shows on TV are about entertainment and they're never about talent. But right from the off I could tell this was different, it was all about the voice and I wanted to do it because I love singing so much.

It was my mum who'd heard about it first, she texted me some details when

I was at work one night and I had a good feeling about it. I really wasn't happy stacking shelves, so I decided to give it up and focus on this, which was such a relief but at the same time I was risking everything. That job was my only regular income apart from some gigging here and there.

'It was such a relief but I was risking everything'

When I got the phone call just before Christmas saying I was through to the Blind Auditions I was ecstatic. It was like the best Christmas present and a brilliant way to start the new year. The first person I called was my mum and it was such a relief to know I hadn't quit my job for a silly dream and that something good had come out of it. I'm still getting my head around it to be honest!'

THE VOICES THAT INSPIRE ME

At the moment I'm really into James Vincent McMorrow – he has such a good voice and always sings in falsetto. I love Del Amitri too, they were the band that inspired me to write songs.

TEAM DANNY

READY FOR
BATTLE?

As the serious matter of vocal sessions for the Battles got underway at a top secret London location, we caught up with the rival coaches to find out why they're convinced their artists have got what it takes to go all the way...

TEAM DANNY

◀ Bo Bruce & Vince Freeman

'Bo has the type of voice that's going to sell millions of records and that's why I picked her. Vince had a great rock voice, he's a down to earth lad and a fantastic vocalist.'

◀ Max Milner & Bill Downs

'Max was the first artist I picked for my team because I was impressed by the mash-up he put together and because he sang like he meant it. Bill was just a great singer, he's got a very good falsetto and the ladies love him.'

◀ Murray Hockridge & Hannah Berney

'I heard Murray busking about six years ago on Grafton Street in Dublin, so it was really spooky to suddenly hear that voice again at the audition. I love the worn smoky wisdom of his voice. Hannah is my powerhouse singer. She's a great vocalist with lots of tricks in her bag.'

◀ David Julien & John James Newman

'David sang my song 'The Man Who Can't Be Moved' at the Blinds which was a ballsy move, but he had the voice to carry it through. He had a great tone to his voice. John James is the consummate professional, a great vocalist and performer. At the audition I don't think there was one note that was out.'

◀ Aleks Josh & Emmy J Mac

'Aleks had me and will.i.am turn around in the first couple of bars, because he's got a great natural voice. Emmy had a lovely tone to her voice and singing 'Put Your Records On' at the audition was a great choice to demonstrate what she can do.'

GUEST ADVISOR

Paloma Faith

In 2009 the British singer-songwriter (and sometime-actress) released her platinum-selling debut *Do You Want The Truth Or Something Beautiful?*. It remained in the album charts for over 40 weeks and included the hits 'Stone Cold Sober' and 'New York'.

◀ David Faulkner & Cassius Henry

'David was one of the first people I turned around for at the Blinds, because I heard so much energy in his performance and his licks were amazing. As for Cassius, I loved that I could hear the need for us to turn around in his voice. He was really working for it and some of his vocal ability was just amazing.'

◀ Indie and Pixie & Becky Hill

'Indie and Pixie are real characters and that comes across when they sing. Becky's voice, I literally melted for her. There was an honesty about her performance which I loved.'

◀ Vince Kidd & Jessica Hammond

'They both very much did their own spin on their songs at the auditions. They're both so completely unique and have their own vibes. And that's why I put them together, because I wanted them to bring the best out of each other.'

◀ Ben Kelly & Ruth Ann St Luce

'Ben's performance at the Blinds was one of the most entertaining. He's very quirky and very much an artist who knows himself. I heard so much diamond in Ruth Ann's voice. She's somebody that has been blessed with a talent and it needs to be nurtured.'

◀ Kirsten Joy & Toni Warne

'Toni and Kirsten are two massive vocalists. Kirsten I only heard sing very high in her chest belt and for someone to sustain that for 90 seconds, well I was very impressed. Toni is a storyteller, I got goosebumps listening to her.'

GUEST ADVISOR
Anna Matronic

The female singer of the New York based Scissor Sisters burst onto the UK music scene alongside her bandmates in 2003. The group's first albums hit the top spot and 2010's *Night Work* reached No 2. Their single 'I Don't Feel Like Dancin'' was a European smash and a UK No 1.

TEAM WILL.I.AM

◀ Joelle Moses & Jenny Jones

'I needed Joelle on my squad because I wanted that calibre of singer – so I could learn from her! She is top notch, one of those undeniable singers. As is Jenny. She's a total powerhouse, they're both powerhouses and that's why I wanted them to sing together.'

◀ Sophie Griffin & J Marie Cooper

'Sophie had this cool little attitude going on when she sang at the audition and she sings amazingly. J Marie – that's a star. She has great control and amazing clarity. She's powerful enough that she can throw in some moves and still control her breathing.'

◀ Jay Norton & Jaz Ellington

'Jay is a quirky guy, he's got a unique little perspective and his singing is amazing. Meanwhile Jaz has a lovely voice. I'm trying to think what instrument he sounds like, maybe an alto sax or an oboe? His voice is so warm.'

◀ Tyler James & Heshima Thompson

'Tyler is a star. I liked how smooth he was at the Blinds, such a cool guy and his falsetto was amazing. Heshima has a proper R 'n' B soul voice and a personality that really shines through.'

◀ Frances Wood & Kate Read

'Frances is like a switchblade, she can sing in any style. She reminds me of someone we would've hung out with in LA, she would've been one of our crew. Kate's style is very much to my personal taste. I don't like singers who do lots of crazy runs, all that wailing is a turn-off for me. I like singers who sing from the heart like Kate.'

GUEST ADVISOR

Dante Santiago

Often referred to as the fifth pea in The Black Eyed Peas, Dante is the creative A&R for will.i.am's music label. He remains one of his closest collaborators and has featured on *Songs About Girls*, Fergie's *The Dutchess* and many Peas' megahits.

TEAM TOM JONES

◀ Aundrea Nyle & Sam Buttery

'Aundrea was the very first person to audition but the power of her voice impressed me so much I turned round. Her vibrato was spot on. Sam has a great range and there were certain notes he hit that reminded me of myself. He had a lot of attack and you could tell he was giving it the full monty.'

◀ Barbara Bryceland & Leanne Mitchell

'Barbara has a hell of a voice, she has a full-on boom and the audience took to her straight away. Leanne also impressed me at the Blinds because again she has a strong voice, quite a deep voice. She came on and she attacked it.'

◀ Matt and Sueleen & Lindsey Butler

'I picked Matt and Sueleen because they sounded so fresh and different and I thought the notes Sueleen picked for the harmonies were really good. Lindsey had her own sense of individuality about her voice which really appealed to me.'

◀ Deniece Pearson & Ruth Brown

'It was Deniece's tone and power that hit me straight away and at the audition she came out with a high note which was just tremendous. Ruth has got a big, open, impressive voice too. They are both very soulful but in different ways.'

◀ Adam Isaac & Denise Morgan

'Adam's voice was very fresh and he had a gravelly quality about him which I really liked. While I wasn't looking for a specific voice, it had to have character and Denise has a fragility in her voice which was very appealing.'

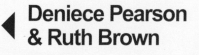

GUEST ADVISOR

Cerys Matthews

As lead singer with Welsh rock band Catatonia, Cerys topped the charts with the multi-platinum-selling albums *International Velvet* and *Equally Cursed And Blessed*. She duetted with our very own Tom Jones on 'Baby, It's Cold Outside' and released her debut solo album in 2003.

Ruth Brown

Once I got on stage I just told myself to calm down and enjoy it and I really did. It was amazing. Then at the end I had my eyes closed and I didn't realise that Tom had turned round right at the last minute – so at first I thought I hadn't got through then I realised I had!

This 20-year-old Londoner is a shy girl with a huge sound – for her *The Voice* is an opportunity to blossom as a performer...

'I once sang for the Prime Minister inside 10 Downing Street for Peace Week, that was quite nerve-racking but it was nothing compared to singing on *The Voice*. I remember on the day of the Blinds I was so nervous I just wanted to get it over with. I'm not really someone who likes being centre of attention, I'm quiet really, so when I start to sing people are always surprised by this big voice that comes out of me.

'People are always surprised by this big voice that comes out of me'

When I came off stage my sisters just kept saying my dad would've been really proud. He passed away a few weeks before the audition so it was all quite overwhelming. My dad taught me the piano when I was seven, which I now use to help with my songwriting and he knew all about *The Voice*. When I sing I'm singing for him.'

THE VOICES THAT INSPIRE ME

I always listen to Adele's *21*. Her singing isn't fake, you can hear the rawness in her voice. I love Jennifer Hudson and Whitney Houston too, they both sing with real emotion.

TEAM TOM JONES

Cassius Henry

The Blind Audition was the first time I had been on stage for around six years, so that was a big deal for me. I don't know why, people kept asking me to perform, but I think my motivation had just disappeared. Being back on stage for *The Voice* – even though I felt a bit rusty – reminded me what I love about performing.

At 16 years old, Cassius was on his way to becoming a successful R&B star, but when his brother tragically died his world fell apart. Now the 32-year-old South Londoner is back doing what he does best...

'This is a second chance for me, it hasn't been an easy journey but now I feel ready to grab this opportunity. When someone close to you passes away and when you have disappointments in your career, you lose your mojo. The confidence fades and you need time to sort your head out.

'I've definitely got my mojo back'

Then to have both Jessie and Danny, people you respect as musicians, turning around and the fact they are intrigued by your voice in some way, that was such a cool thing. The calibre in this competition is so high that mentally you have to focus 100 per cent, so I am really feeling that sense of drive again. I've definitely got my mojo back.'

THE VOICES THAT INSPIRE ME

Stevie Wonder. I'm basically a soul singer and his is the only male voice that has made me feel something quiver inside. I'm listening to a lot of Adele too – now that's a voice!

TEAM JESSIE J

THE BATTLES

The gloves were off as the artists duelled against each other for a coveted place in the live shows. Here's our round-up of the knockout performances...

Two artists, one boxing-ring

style set and some very difficult decisions for the coaches. Over the next two days the formidable performers who made it through the Blind Auditions sang for survival against a fellow member of their talented team. And of course we had an exclusive ring-side seat, with hand-towels at the ready in case anyone needed their sweaty brow mopping (okay, we made that last bit up).

The first artists exchanging vocal blows were flat-cap-wearer Murray Hockridge (above, left) and sometime-cheerleader Hannah Berney (above, right), who got the party started with their crowd-pleasing take on Robbie Williams and Kylie Minogue's 'Kids'. According to will.i.am their high notes were 'freaking amazing' while Murray's more experienced voice edged it for Sir Tom. But it's their mentor Danny who has the final say and he's seriously flummoxed. 'I like both of you, so this is very hard,' he says, playing with his quiff as he chews it over. He eventually decides to take Hannah through to the next stage, but Murray is gracious in defeat: 'All I can say is it has been a pleasure to perform in front of you guys.'

Next up for Team will.i.am are 'triple-threat' entertainer Heshima Thompson (below, left) and Tyler James (below, right), who's looking very dapper in a checked Bugsy Malone style jacket. Their souled-up version of Chris Brown's 'Yeah 3X' is hard to call. Jessie J says she'd go with Heshima because of his 'amazing vocals', but at the same time she loved the way Tyler

put his own spin on it. Meanwhile their coach is deep in thought. 'I am proud of both of you guys,' will.i.am tells them. 'Tyler you knocked me out with your performance and Heshima every lick was incredible. So this is hard. But I'm going to go for someone who was thrown an obstacle and knew how to own it.' And he names Tyler as his battle-winner.

Two very different artists are up against each other next – heartfelt performer Ruth-Ann St Luce (far right) and Ben Kelly (right), who has a quirky style all of his own. Tom rates them 'equally as strong as each other' on 'I Wanna Dance With Somebody'. Danny agrees they both 'smashed it'. Even their coach Jessie J is stumped. 'Boy, why did I put you two together?' she asks herself. 'Ben, your upper range is unstoppable,' she adds, before finally settling on Ruth-Ann as her choice for the live shows.

Barbara Bryceland (below, left) and Leanne Mitchell (below, right) blow the roof off with their vocals on 'Edge Of Glory' and all four coaches jump to their feet. An impressed Danny says Barbara brought the house down, while Leanne's vocal licks made the hairs on the back

Meanwhile the duo's coach has tears in his eyes. 'This is really difficult. The hardest thing I have ever done in my life,' reveals Tom. 'It's a very tough decision because you are both powerhouses. I feel I've got the strongest voices

of his neck stand up. will.i.am mischievously asks Barbara if she was singing to him. 'I think I've got a crush on Barbara right now,' he grins.

on the show so this is really difficult for me'. After much soul-searching, it's a delighted Leanne that he puts through to the next round.

Coach Danny gives Bo Bruce (right) and Vince Freeman (far right, who is once again shoeless) a big thumbs up as they begin 'With Or Without You' and their intense vocals soar beautifully. Jessie reveals she was 'literally hypnotised' by their performance. will.i.am says they are both superstars and Tom adds he'd like to hear them record an album together. Danny tells Vince: 'From day one you have been a perfect, immaculate, incredible vocalist. You're a better singer than I am.' But Danny picks Bo, saying: 'When you open your voice, magic happens.'

The crowd go wild for David Faulkner (left) and Cassius Henry's (far left) 'Beat It' and their coach Jessie J shimmies along in her seat. 'You are two of the nicest guys I've met because you are so humble with your talent,' she says, clearly moved and dabbing her eyes to stop her make-up running. 'I was tough in rehearsal but I'm so proud of both of you.' She chooses Cassius as the battle winner before giving David a big hug as he leaves the stage.

Joelle Moses (far right) and Jenny Jones (right) get their fiery vocal chops around 'I'm Every Woman' and the audience love their diva-licious hand-flicking attitude. 'It's a tough decision,' admits Jessie. 'You both have different qualities and sounds and bring different flavours to the song. I can't pick because you both have something special.' And it seems their mentor will.i.am can't decide either – in the end he puts a very happy Joelle through to the live rounds.

Tom is also in a quandary after Adam Isaac (below, right) and new mum Denise Morgan's (below, left) storming version of 'Use Somebody'. 'You both did such a great job so again this is the difficult part for me.' Ultimately he goes with a relieved Adam, but Denise is gallant in defeat and everyone agrees her son Gabriel will be very proud of his mum.

By the end all the coaches are on their feet and Danny admits he's been blown away by their showmanship. 'It was a stupid thing to do to put you both together. I thought it was the battle of the night! Bill, you are unstoppable now. This is so difficult, but I am going to go with my gut...' and he chooses a grateful Max as the one that he wants.

It's a battle of two cool dudes for Team Danny. Trilbied Max Milner (below, left) and tattooed Bill Downs (below, right) amicably tap fists then get right into each other's faces as they swagger through an adrenalised 'Beggin' by Madcon.

Meanwhile the reaction of the crowd to Kirsten Joy (above, right) and Toni Warne's (above, left) vocal acrobatics on 'Think' is almost deafening. A dazzled will.i.am says: 'I never thought that two voices could sound like a choir. Toni you

have so much grace, power and pain and love in your voice. And Kirsten every note, every lick was amazing. You're like Ninja Assassin Singers!' Their coach Jessie J agrees. 'You are two of the best female voices I have heard in the UK. I would be scared to sing with you guys because there was not one note out. It's going to be a tough decision for me, but it was an honour for us to hear you both sing.' Eventually she picks Toni as her winner citing the 'story in her voice.'

belt out 'Firework', but are all smiles and have a big friendly hug as they wait for their feedback. 'There were certainly some fireworks on stage just there. It was a battle of youth against experience,' says Tom, before adding that if it was down to him he would name J Marie as the victor. Coach will.i.am looks sombre as he explains he can relate to both of their situations, but opts to go with 'the person I was at 17' and picks a stunned Sophie.

It's two against one when Matt and Sueleen (above, right) take on Lindsey Butler (above, left) for a spirited rendition of 'Born To Run'. An impressed Jessie makes the point that the show isn't about winners and losers, it's about showing talent. But it's Tom who has the final say. 'You are all great in your own ways. Matt and Sueleen you have great harmonies and Lindsey you have a very unique sounding voice. All three of you are fantastic, but the act I am choosing as the winner of this battle is... Matt & Sueleen.'

Experienced backing singer J Marie Cooper (left) and 17-year-old Sophie Griffin (right) give each other loads of in your face attitude as they

will.i.am's smiley face is back for the next duet and he congratulates Indie & Pixie (opposite, left) after their battle with Becky Hill (opposite, right) on Beyoncé's 'Irreplaceable'. 'You were a 100 gazillion per cent better than you guys did at the audition. Especially as you were going up against Becky The Vampire Slayer!' he adds, laughing. Their coach Jessie also comments on the duo's improvement, but ultimately selects Becky as her battle-winner because of the 'power and passion' in her voice.

David Julien (opposite, above left) and John James Newman (opposite, above right) work up quite a sweat and are clearly having a ball as they rock-out to 'Dakota' by the Stereophonics. 'You entertained my life,' laughs Jessie. Meanwhile Tom says his mate Kelly Jones would've loved their

version. 'My heart is going 90 miles per hour at the moment,' says their coach Danny. 'This is the hardest decision I have ever had to make probably in my life...' In the end he picks David with a big compliment: 'I hear things in your voice I wish I had in mine.'

The audience goes wild as former Five Star lead singer Deniece Pearson (above, left) and 20-year-old Ruth Brown (above, right) attempt to outdo each other on Alicia Keys' 'No One'. The pair give an impassioned vocal masterclass and their mentor Tom Jones's eyes fill with tears during their performance. Danny is blown away. 'That was amazing, I think I heard every note ever created in the last two minutes.'

will.i.am says Deniece reminds him of superstars like Whitney Houston and Michael Jackson, while Ruth impressed him by singing from the soul. Tom still looks shaken. 'This is a very emotional experience... the standard and power of that was unbelievable. I could feel so much soul from both of you.' After pausing again for a moment he chooses Ruth, who falls to her knees with joy.

people, so it's hard because it feels like I'm saying goodbye to friends. Kate has the kind of voice I like to listen to, like Sade or Macy Gray.' Eventually he puts 'vocal chameleon' Frances through to the next round.

'I don't envy you,' says Tom, when Jessie has to decide between Vince Kidd (bottom, left) and Jessica Hammond (bottom, right) after they've had the whole studio audience on their feet with Rihanna's 'We Found Love'. 'You've picked two crackers there,' he adds. Jessie is torn, 'This is tough.com!' she says, stealing one of will.i.am's catchphrases. In the end she goes with Vince, explaining she can imagine people going to see him in concert.

Jessie J says she is lost for words after Frances Wood (above, left) and Kate Read's (above, right) version of Alanis Morissette's 'Ironic' – which Tom cheekily points out makes a change. Their mentor will.i.am admits he has a tricky choice to make. 'You are both my favourite

will.i.am loves Aleks Josh (above, left) and Emmy J Mac's (above, right) take on 'Broken Strings' and compliments their 'amazing voices', while Jessie says their performance was like watching a music video and she wanted them to kiss at the end! Aaah. Although Emmy doesn't think her boyfriend would be too keen about

Finally Jay Norton (below, left) and Jaz Ellington (below, right) turn up the heat for Team will.i.am with a soulful 'I Heard It Through The Grapevine'. The coaches give them a standing ovation and this time they remain on their feet to give their feedback. Jessie says she's lost for words at how good it was, adding 'I'm just glad the world got the chance to hear you both sing.' Meanwhile Danny is equally enthused. 'This is what *The Voice* is all about and that's why I'm still standing.'

that. It's their mentor Danny who has the final say. 'I am so proud of how far you have both come. Nerves can get the better of you, Aleks, I still get nervous even now. Emmy you have a really unique tone and a great voice.' After much deliberation he picks Aleks because 'he still has so much to show'.

Tom Jones super-fan Sam Buttery (above, left) and Aundrea Nyle (above, right looking resplendent in a feather neck-lined top) vigorously storm their way through 'A Little Less Conversation', which is perfect for Sam as he already has the Elvis quiff going on. Danny gives them a standing ovation. 'Now that's what I call a battle!' he exclaims. 'You are both brilliant singers and entertainers.' will.i.am is equally rapturous. 'My eyebrows were so far back I had to take them out of my back pocket and put them back on my head.' Proud coach Tom describes it as an incredibly sassy performance. 'I've loved working with both of you in rehearsal.' In the end he names Sam as the victor who seems flabbergasted at being chosen. 'Am I really through?' he asks.

Knowing this decision is going to be a toughie, a thoughtful-looking will.i.am pauses for a moment before saying his piece. 'Jaz, you have so much soul and vocal talent and range. Jay, your riffs are out of this world. You are better

than Justin Timberlake at what you do.' But Jaz is the one he's selecting to go through to the next phase of the competition. He explains why: 'I want to take Jaz to the lives because you got soul in a bowl, soul on a pole!' And you can't say fairer than that...

Frances Wood

because I'm gigging all the time, but my friends understand how much it means to me. I have honestly worked so hard to get to this point and if I have to work 1000 times harder than I have been to be successful then I'll do it.

Getting onto *The Voice* has been brilliant and being on will.i.am's team is so cool. I was quite worried about singing 'Where Is The Love' at the audition because I thought if will.i.am doesn't turn around, i.e the person who originally did the song, then I'll know I've done a really bad job. So when nobody pressed their buzzer I was just trying to stay positive and think "Oh well, I've done pretty well to get this far out of the thousands who auditioned." Then will.i.am literally turned around on the last note – I thought "Oh you cheeky wotsit." But it was the best feeling in the world!'

The 18-year-old performing arts student spends every weekend busking and gigging around her hometown of Wakefield to raise money for piano and singing lessons...

'I busk, I gig, I play piano, I write my own songs – everything I do is based around music. I can't imagine a life where I'm not singing. I know sometimes I miss out on other stuff

'I can't imagine a life where I'm not singing'

THE VOICES THAT INSPIRE ME

I love Rihanna and Birdy – they are very different artists but both have something unique about their vocals. I like voices with character and I love Matthew Murphy of The Wombats.

TEAM WILL.I.AM

The 17-year-old part-time lifeguard's ambition has always been to make a career out of his love of music. But after getting through the Blinds it took a hug from Jessie J for it all to sink in...

'I wouldn't say I was bad at school, my problem was that I was always questioning the teachers and asking why we had to do stuff. In my eyes I just wanted to be a singer so I didn't

'The whole thing felt like an out of body experience'

understand what science lessons or maths were going to add to my singing voice. I can see now it wasn't a great attitude.

I used to sing as a hobby doing theatre and I've done some demos, but nothing could've prepared me for *The Voice*. This has been a whole different ballgame altogether, a totally surreal but brilliant experience.

I was so nervous before the Blinds that my mouth kept drying up and I drank so much water. I was literally shaking as I walked on because I was really scared that I'd muck up. So when will.i.am and Danny both turned round I was lost for words. I was totally overawed by it and next thing I knew Jessie J was sitting next to me on the stage giving me a hug. The whole thing felt like an out of body experience.'

THE VOICES THAT INSPIRE ME

I like a lot of folk music like Simon & Garfunkel. They tell amazing stories with their voices and their harmonies are just so creative. Donovan is another big influence on me.

TEAM DANNY

MEET
THE BAND

The Voice's musical director Steve Sidwell is a musician, composer, arranger and conductor whose orchestrations and compositions have appeared on albums and movie soundtracks galore...

He's played alongside greats such as George Michael, Paul McCartney, Amy Winehouse and Robbie Williams, and he's even performed his own specially commissioned piece in front of Hollywood's finest on stage at the Academy Awards. Here Steve (pictured third from right) gives us the inside story on the hardest working band in television....

'When I was asked to be the musical director on the show I did some research and watched as much as I could of the American version. And I liked what I saw. Music seemed to be the main focus, which as a musician really appealed to me.

So the first thing I had to do was form a band. The producers wanted it to feel like a rock 'n'roll band, something outside of the regular telly bands where people are sitting there with music stands and a conductor. They wanted us to feel like the kind of band you see at gigs, with a lot of stuff committed to memory instead of written down on sheets in front of us. So that was an interesting challenge and it was more like putting a band together for a rock 'n'roll tour than a TV series.

I went for people who'd been involved in both the session world and the rock 'n'roll world. It's no good having musicians there who can only play one kind of music, because on *The Voice* we've got to cover pretty much every musical genre you've ever heard of. Over the Blind Auditions we covered everything from opera to techno, so I needed people who were capable of playing pretty much everything, yet would still feel comfortable in a rock 'n'roll style line-up.

Once the songs have been chosen it's my job to do the 90-second 'cut-downs'(shortened versions of the songs) for each stage of the competition. Of course, cut-downs are difficult to do because people write these songs for a reason and for whoever wrote the song, that whole three and a half minutes means something to them. And then someone like me comes along and chops their work in half.

Actually, it was interesting talking to Danny O'Donoghue the other day, who was saying he doesn't usually like people cutting down his songs and I said to him: "Danny, didn't you notice I cut down two of your songs in the show?"And he said: "Yeah, they were great!" I managed to get them past Danny so I guess they must've been okay. The trick is to have the main elements of the song that people expect to hear, combined with a chance for the singer to show off the best of themselves, all in 90 seconds. It's a challenge because you need to cover as many aspects of the song as possible, but for it still to stand up as a piece of music.

'It was more like putting a band together for a rock 'n' roll tour than a TV series'

The Blind Auditions were an incredibly intense period of work. We had seven days of band rehearsal followed by seven days of rehearsals with the contestants. Then we had three days of rehearsal in the studio. Apart from the 105 or so songs we played during the actual auditions, there were other songs we'd learnt that had been rejected or that we'd had to learn just in case there were any last minute changes. So I think in total for the Blinds we had to learn 167 songs, which is no mean feat.

We pretty much learn everything to memory band-style in that we aren't sight reading. But we did use iPads for notes because I think to learn that much in the time we had wasn't feasible without the odd prompt. We also had to programme in various electronic elements, because there are some sounds you can't necessarily replicate with a live band.

On the morning of the Blind Audition days we'd come in and sound check for an hour at midday, then we'd start recording at two in the afternoon. If we're lucky we'd get a 40-minute break for tea, but apart from that we'd be recording an audition every ten minutes or so until around nine or ten in the evening.

The behind-the-scenes process was that before each act came on to audition our Pro Tools operator would play us the songs as we did them in rehearsal in our headphones, we'd listen once through, make some mental notes and then we'd go ahead and play them. So we literally just had a 90-second reminder before the next act came on of what we had to do. Luckily nothing went wrong – I'm not quite sure how that happened!

Some of the performers do get nervous and part of my role is to put people at their ease, calm them down and make them feel comfortable musically. It's a matter of making sure they know what they are doing, what their introduction is and that they can hear themselves. I try to make sure I look after the contestants as best I can.

There's definitely some stand-out talent on the show. It's always a thrill to work with talented people and see them rise to the occasion and enjoy performing with the band. And it's always a thrill for me to play with the great musicians we have in the band, because these guys are the best players you'll find anywhere.

Pete Murray is an amazing piano player, Jerry Meehan is Robbie Williams' bass player and he co-wrote *Rudebox* with him, Adam Goldsmith's the hot new guy in town and he's a great guitarist, while Ian Thomas is a seasoned performer – he has been Seal's drummer, Mark Knopfler's drummer, Eric Clapton's drummer and he's always my first choice. Lester Salmins works on the cut-downs with me, David Hearn and Dave Walter are the Pro Tools programmers and Richard Sidwell, my brother, helps me with the arrangements and does all the music preparation – so he has been a very busy guy.

'In total for the Blinds we had to learn 167 songs, which is no mean feat'

After the intensity of the Blinds I think we were all tired. But I didn't really stop because I had to start thinking about the Battles, working on the song choices and doing the cut-downs. All the coaches on the show are amazing so it's great to be able to work closely with all of them. With the Battles you have the added complication in that they are duets so you've got to decide, along with the coaches, who sings which bit of each song and then arrange any harmonies. So there's a lot to do in between the recording days. It has been pretty exhausting – but it's always a lot of fun.'

Sam Buttery

The 20-year-old big-voiced Brummie has deferred his place at university to concentrate on his love of music and to learn from his idol Tom Jones...

'I have listened to Tom Jones ever since I was a kid. I love his funky soul stuff like 'Black Betty' and his brilliant version of 'I Who Have Nothing'. So when he turned around for me at the Blinds I was really happy. When he said that my voice reminded him a little bit of his, well, I was blown away. That's made my year. Actually it has made my life.

While rehearsing for the Battles I had to tell Tom how I felt about him. To be in the same room as your idol is unbelievable and just really emotional. At one point I had a little tear drop down my cheek.

'To be in the same room as your idol is emotional'

Before *The Voice* I'd done some musical theatre at uni and was just starting to find my feet at open-mike sessions. I probably haven't got as much experience as some of the others here, but I'm learning more each day. Danny said he thought he was listening to a female voice when he first heard me and I always have people telling me they expect to see a big black gospel songstress when they hear me sing – but it's just little old me!'

THE VOICES THAT INSPIRE ME

I love Roy Orbison. He's got an amazing warble to his voice that really gets you in the heart. Elvis Presley and Lady Gaga are big favourites too – they are both so unique.

TEAM TOM JONES

Somehow I got there and I just had to do the best I could under the circumstances. They all seemed to enjoy my performance and when I got asked to try another song by Jessie I randomly started singing 'Ordinary

'I can't describe it any better than as a fairytale moment'

Everything the 27-year-old gospel singer from South East London does revolves around singing – but he didn't expect his voice to move will.i.am and Jessie J to tears...

'I had no idea I was going to get that reaction. I can't describe it any better than to say it felt like a Disney fairytale moment. I'd been in and out of hospital the whole week of the Blind Auditions. I had two massive asthma attacks and I remember lying on a hospital bed with a nebuliser in my mouth and saying to my wife "Do you know what, I bet I'm not even going to make it to audition."

People', mainly because I knew the words. Then Jessie started crying and then I noticed Will was crying too. That's the point at which I thought, what's happening here?

It was a big shock for me that I could touch them like that with my voice, I mean these are people whose music I listen to at home on my iPod all the time. It was so humbling – I really will never forget that moment.'

THE VOICES THAT INSPIRE ME

I don't think I'd be able to sing the way I do if I hadn't been listening to Whitney Houston. Her voice has complete heart and passion. Stevie Wonder is another ridiculously great inspiration.

TEAM
WILL. I. AM

LIVING

As Tom Jones enjoys his sixth decade in the music business, we celebrate the life of an iconic star...

Even as a child Thomas Woodward loves singing for his parents, Freda and Thomas, and assorted relatives at their home in Pontypridd, South Wales: 'Some kids they're shy. Me though, I was always dying to get up to sing. And I would get attention for it and a response, so of course I loved it all the more.' He works on building sites as a labourer and in 1957 he marries childhood sweetheart, Linda, and they have a son, Mark.

He begins his music career as vocalist in the beat group Tommy Scott & The Senators. In 1964 he changes his name to Tom Jones and heads for London with manager Gordon Mills. His first single, 'Chills and Fever', fails to chart. But his second, 'It's Not Unusual', is an international smash: 'As soon as I heard "It's Not Unusual" I thought – my God that song has some magic to it.'

LEGEND

By 1965 he's mixing with the likes of The Beatles and Dusty Springfield, opening for the Rolling Stones and performing movie title tracks such as 'Thunderball'. Legend has it the final note of the Bond song is so high he faints while recording it. In 1969 he signs a megabucks deal for his TV show, *This Is Tom Jones*, which airs on both sides of the Atlantic – guests include Janis Joplin, Johnny Cash and fellow Welsh warbler Shirley Bassey.

Having rocketed to fame, Tom's childhood idol Elvis Presley requests to meet him in Hollywood: 'I thought, my God. I didn't know that he knew that I existed, because I only had three singles out and one album at the time. When I go on the set where Elvis was filming, he walked towards me singing "With These Hands", which was my record. I couldn't believe it. We became friends from that day on and we were friends until just before he died.'

In 1974 he revisits his birthplace in 'Ponty'. But his return is much more high-profile in 2005 with a homecoming gig in front of 20,000 fans. The last time he'd played the town was in the early 60s in a pub with Tommy Scott & The Senators.

He celebrates his 38th birthday in Las Vegas with pals including Joan Rivers, Sonny Bono and Dionne Warwick. While headlining at Caesar's Palace his snake-hipped thrusting and tight trousers drive fans wild: 'At that point I don't think people cared about what I was singing, as long as I had tight pants and they could throw knickers at me. That overtook the talent which I never meant for it to do.'

In 1986 following the sad death of Gordon Mills, Tom's son Mark takes over as his manager. Out goes the knicker-grabbing showmanship and in comes a change of direction. Two years later, Tom and avant-garde synth-group, Art Of Noise, have a massive hit with the Prince song, 'Kiss', and a new younger generation join Team Tom.

Performing with Robbie Williams at the Brit Awards in 1998 leads to *Reload*, an album of covers with other artists including Robbie, Stereophonics and The Cardigans. It's the biggest hit of his career selling a whopping four million copies worldwide.

Arise Sir Tom! In 2006 he is knighted by the Queen at Buckingham Palace: 'That was probably the biggest thing that's ever happened to me. It's a pinnacle. It was mind-boggling to me. I was shaking when they told me I was being considered.'

In 2009 he joins *Gavin & Stacey*'s Ruth Jones and Rob Brydon for the No 1 Comic Relief single 'Barry Islands In The Stream': 'I had a lot of fun with it. I was already a fan of the series. When I met Ruth I told her I thought Nessa had a perfect Barry accent, but Stacey's was a bit too Swansea. She told me only the Welsh knew. I knew alright.'

Nearly 50 years since the release of 'It's Not Unusual', Tom wows the crowds on the main stage at T in the Park in 2011 with highlights from his recent gospel and blues-tinged album *Praise & Blame* – plus there's a sun-kissed sing-a-long to classics 'Delilah' and 'Leave Your Hat On'. We salute you Sir!

ARE YOU THEBOMB.COM OR JUST REDONKULOUS?

Find out which coach you are by answering this probing personality test...

1. **When you open your eyes in the morning what's your very first thought?**

   a) I got a feeling (woo-hoo) that today's gonna be a good day. That today's gonna be a good day. Today's gonna be a good good day

   b) Eeek, I need to backcomb my quiff

   c) My fringe has gone wonky, but it's okay not to be okay

   d) What's new pussycat?

2. **What is your favourite item of clothing?**

   a) Cycling gloves (especially when not cycling)

   b) Double Denim

   c) It's all about the sky-high heels

   d) You can't beat a black turtle-neck

3. **What's the one thing you would demand to have in your dressing room at all times?**

   a) An endless supply of (black-eyed) peas

   b) Your guitar – there's the new album to think about

   c) Your mobile phone – the 'Heartbeats' need you to keep in touch

   d) A Welsh Male Voice Choir. Or maybe some leeks?

4. **You are handed the bill after a meal in a top restaurant, what do you say to the waiter?**

   a) That you loved their soul in a bowl

   b) Complain there wasn't any coddle or fadge on the menu

   c) It's not about the money, money, money!

   d) That you and Elvis used to eat burgers together

ARE YOU THEBOMB.COM OR JUST REDONKULOUS?

Find out which coach you are by answering this probing personality test...

1. **When you open your eyes in the morning what's your very first thought?**
   a) I got a feeling (woo-hoo) that today's gonna be a good day. That today's gonna be a good day. Today's gonna be a good good day
   b) Eeek, I need to backcomb my quiff
   c) My fringe has gone wonky, but it's okay not to be okay
   d) What's new pussycat?

2. **What is your favourite item of clothing?**
   a) Cycling gloves (especially when not cycling)
   b) Double Denim
   c) It's all about the sky-high heels
   d) You can't beat a black turtle-neck

3. **What's the one thing you would demand to have in your dressing room at all times?**
   a) An endless supply of (black-eyed) peas
   b) Your guitar – there's the new album to think about
   c) Your mobile phone – the 'Heartbeats' need you to keep in touch
   d) A Welsh Male Voice Choir. Or maybe some leeks?

4. **You are handed the bill after a meal in a top restaurant, what do you say to the waiter?**
   a) That you loved their soul in a bowl
   b) Complain there wasn't any coddle or fadge on the menu
   c) It's not about the money, money, money!
   d) That you and Elvis used to eat burgers together

Nearly 50 years since the release of 'It's Not Unusual', Tom wows the crowds on the main stage at T in the Park in 2011 with highlights from his recent gospel and blues-tinged album *Praise & Blame* – plus there's a sun-kissed sing-a-long to classics 'Delilah' and 'Leave Your Hat On'. We salute you Sir!

5. **You are asked to describe yourself in an interview, what do you say?**
   a) I can describe myself in 3 Words
   b) A Man Who Can't Be Moved
   c) I Do It Like A Dude
   d) A Boy From Nowhere

6. **One of your entourage attempts to talk to you during your favourite TV show, how do you react?**
   a) Tell them to shut up, just shut up, shut up, shut up, just shut up, shut up
   b) Have them removed – no-one is allowed to speak during *Mrs Brown's Boys*!
   c) Just laugh because nobody's perfect
   d) Shrug your shoulders, it's not unusual for this to happen

7. **At a family party your four-year-old niece starts singing 'Twinkle Twinkle Little Star'. What do you say to her?**
   a) You're the bomb.com!
   b) You have a great tone but the song choice let you down
   c) You're redonkulous! But you need to work on your breathing and diction
   d) Explain you liked it, but prefer Elvis's version

8. **So, the series is over. What's the first thing you do?**
   a) Celebrate at Mahiki with your bezzie Cheryl Cole
   b) Get on the first plane to Dublin
   c) Twitter your fans about it of course!
   d) Head for the Green Green Grass Of Home

YOU ARE A DEAD-RINGER FOR...

Mostly A's
You're the bomb.com!
You are music mogul: WILL.I.AM

Mostly B's
Irish eyes are smiling! According to this Script you are: DANNY O'DONOGHUE

Mostly C's
Forget about the Price Tag!
You are London's finest diva: JESSIE J

Mostly D's
Cooler than an igloo! You are the legend himself: TOM JONES